D0536466

I2618681

WALKING INTO HELL

THE SOMME THROUGH BRITISH AND GERMAN EYES

EDWARD G. D. LIVEING

&

SIR PHILIP GIBBS

FOREWORD BY
BOB CARRUTHERS

Pen & Sword
MILITARY

This edition published in 2014 by

Pen & Sword Military
An imprint of
Pen & Sword Books Ltd
47 Church Street
Barnsley
South Yorkshire
S70 2AS

Part one of this book was first published as 'Attack: An Infantry Subaltern's Impressions of July 1ˢᵗ 1916'
by The Macmillan Company, New York, 1918.

Part two of this book was first published as 'The Germans On the Somme'
by Darling & Son Ltd., London, 1917.

Copyright © Coda Books Ltd.
Published under licence by Pen & Sword Books Ltd.

ISBN: 9781783463145

A CIP catalogue record for this book is available from the British Library.

All rights reserved. No part of this book may be reproduced or transmitted in any form or by any means,
electronic or mechanical including photocopying, recording or by any information storage and retrieval
system, without permission from the Publisher in writing.

Printed and bound in England
By CPI Group (UK) Ltd, Croydon, CR0 4YY

Pen & Sword Books Ltd incorporates the imprints of Pen & Sword Aviation, Pen & Sword Family
History, Pen & Sword Maritime, Pen & Sword Military, Pen & Sword Discovery, Pen & Sword Politics,
Pen & Sword Atlas, Pen & Sword Archaeology, Wharncliffe Local History, Wharncliffe True Crime,
Wharncliffe Transport, Pen & Sword Select, Pen & Sword Military Classics, Leo Cooper, The Praetorian
Press, Claymore Press, Remember When, Seaforth Publishing and Frontline Publishing

For a complete list of Pen & Sword titles please contact
PEN & SWORD BOOKS LIMITED
47 Church Street, Barnsley, South Yorkshire, S70 2AS, England
E-mail: enquiries@pen-and-sword.co.uk
Website: www.pen-and-sword.co.uk

CONTENTS

FOREWORD

THIS SHORT VOLUME forms part of an occasional series entitled *Military History from Contemporary Sources*. The idea behind the series is to provide the modern reader with a flavour of how these actions were presented to general audiences at the time the events unfolded. I'm pleased to say that the series has been very well received and titles released to date seem to have pleased their readers. This series allows us the opportunity to publish accounts which are too short to form a complete volume but which nonetheless deserve to be more widely read.

This title features a short description of the action on the first day of the Somme by as viewed from the British perspective by Edward G. D. Liveing and a wonderful collection of official war dispatches by Sir Philip Gibbs which were originally published in the *Daily Telegraph* and *Daily Chronicle*.

I find this collection of especial interest as it deals with the both the British experience and also that of the all too often overlooked German Army on the Somme. The events from the British perspective are well represented in the huge volume of reports and autobiographical accounts and, like me, many of our older readers will have heard oral testimony from the participants. However, for English language readers it is much harder to gain an insight into the war as it was experienced from the German side. Gibb's work is welcome therefore as a rare example of a contemporary attempt to view the war from the 'other side of the hill'.

BOB CARRUTHERS

PART I

THE BRITISH EXPERIENCE

BY

EDWARD G. D. LIVEING

TO

THE N.C.O.s

AND

MEN OF No. 5 PLATOON

Of a Battalion of the County of London
Regiment, whom I had the good
fortune to command in France
during 1915-1916, and in
particular to the
memory of

RFN. C. N. DENNISON

My Platoon Observer, who fell in action
July 1st, 1916, in an attempt
to save my life

INTRODUCTION

THE ATTACK ON the fortified village of Gommecourt, which Mr. Liveing describes in these pages with such power and colour, was a part of the first great allied attack on July 1, 1916, which began the Battle of the Somme. That battle, so far as it concerns our own troops, may be divided into two sectors: one, to the south of the Ancre River, a sector of advance, the other, to the north of the Ancre River, a containing sector, in which no advance was possible. Gommecourt itself, which made a slight but important salient in the enemy line in the containing sector, was the most northern point attacked in that first day's fighting.

Though the Gommecourt position is not impressive to lock at, most of our soldiers are agreed that it was one of the very strongest points in the enemy's fortified line on the Western Front. French and Russian officers, who have seen it since the enemy left it, have described it as "terrible" and as "the very devil." There can be no doubt that it was all that they say.

The country in that part is high-lying chalk downland, something like the downland of Berkshire and Buckinghamshire, though generally barer of trees, and less bold in its valleys. Before the war it was cultivated, hedgeless land, under corn and sugar-beet. The chalk is usually well-covered, as in Buckinghamshire, with a fat day. As the French social tendency is all to the community, there are few lonely farms in that countryside as there would be with us. The inhabitants live in many compact villages, each with a church, a market-place, a watering-place for stock, and sometimes a château and park. Most of the villages are built of red brick, and the churches are of stone, not (as in the chalk countries with us) of dressed flint. Nearly all the villages are planted about with orchards; some have copses of timber trees. In general, from any distance, the villages stand out upon the downland as clumps of woodland. Nearly everywhere near the battlefield a clump of orchard, with an occasional dark fir in it, is the mark of some small village. In time of peace the Picardy farming community numbered some two or three hundred souls. Gommecourt and Hébuterne were of the larger kind of village.

A traveller coming towards Gommecourt as Mr. Liveing came to it, from the west, sees nothing of the Gommecourt position till he reaches Hébuterne. It is hidden from him by the tilt of the high-lying chalk plateau, and by the woodland and orchards round Hébuterne village. Passing through this village, which is now deserted, save for a few cats, one comes to a fringe of orchard, now deep in grass, and of exquisite beauty. From the hedge of this fringe of orchard one sees the Gommecourt position straight in front, with the Gommecourt salient curving round on slightly rising ground, so as to enclose the left flank.

At first sight the position is not remarkable. One sees, to the left, a slight rise or swelling in the chalk, covered thickly with the remains and stumps of noble trees, now mostly killed by shell-fire. This swelling, which is covered with the remains of Gommecourt Park, is the salient of the enemy position. The enemy trenches here jut out into a narrow pointing finger to enclose and defend this slight rise.

Further to the right, this rise becomes a low, gentle heave in the chalk, which stretches away to the south for some miles, becoming lower and gentler in its slope as it proceeds. The battered woodland which covers its higher end contains the few stumps and heaps of brick that were once Gommecourt village. The lower end is without trees or buildings.

This slight wooded rise and low, gentle heave in the chalk make up the position of Gommecourt. It is nothing but a gentle rise above a gentle valley. From a mile or two to the south of Gommecourt, this valley appearance becomes more marked. If one looks northward from this point the English lines seem to follow a slight rise parallel with the other. The valley between the two heaves of chalk make the No Man's Land or space between the enemy trenches and our own. The salient shuts in the end of the valley and enfilades it.

The position has changed little since the attack of July 1. Then, as now, Gommecourt was in ruins, and the trees of the wood were mostly killed. Then, as now, the position looked terrible, even though its slopes were gentle and its beauty not quite destroyed, even after two years of war.

The position is immensely strong in itself, with a perfect glacis and field of fire. Every invention of modem defensive war helped to make it stronger. In front of it was the usual system of barbed wire, stretched on iron supports, over a width of fifty yards. Behind the wire was the system of the First Enemy Main Line, from which many communication-trenches ran to the central fortress of the salient, known as the Kern Redoubt, and to the Support or Guard Line. This First Main Line, even now, after countless bombardments and nine months of neglect, is a great and deep trench of immense strength. It is from twelve to fifteen feet deep, very strongly revetted with timberings and stout wicker-work. At intervals it is strengthened with small forts or sentry-boxes of concrete, built into the parapet. Great and deep dugouts lie below it, and though many of these have now been destroyed, the shafts of most of them can still be seen. At the mouths of some of these shafts one may still see giant-legged periscopes by which men sheltered in the dug-out shafts could watch for the coming of an attack. When the attack began and the barrage lifted, these watchers called up the bombers and machine-gunners from their underground barracks, and had them in action within a few seconds.

Though the wire was formidable and the trench immense, the real defences of the position were artillery and machine-guns. The machine-guns were the chief danger. One machine-gun with ample ammunition has concentrated in itself the defensive power of a battalion. The enemy had not less than a dozen machine-guns in and in front of the Kern Redoubt. Some of these were cunningly hidden in pits, tunnels and shelters in (or even outside) the obstacle of the wire at the salient, so that they could enfilade the No Man's Land, or shoot an attacking party in the back after it had passed. The sites of these machine-gun nests were well hidden from all observation, and were frequently changed. Besides the machine-guns outside and in the front line, there were others, mounted in the trees and in the higher ground above the front line, in such position that they, too, could play upon the No Man's Land and the English front line. The artillery concentrated behind Gommecourt was of all calibres. It was a greater concentration than the enemy could then usually afford to defend any one sector, but the number of guns in it is not known. On July 1 it developed a more intense artillery fire upon Hébuterne, and the English line outside it, than upon any part of the English attack throughout the battlefield.

In the attack of July 1, Gommecourt was assaulted simultaneously from the north (from the direction of Fonquevillers) and from the south (from the direction of Hébuterne). Mr. Liveing took part in the southern assault, and must have "gone in" near the Hébuterne-Bucquoy Road. The tactical intention of these simultaneous attacks from north and south was to "pinch off" and secure the salient The attack to the north, though gallantly pushed, was unsuccessful. The attack to the south got across the first-line trench and into the enemy position past Gommecourt Cemetery almost to the Kern Redoubt. What it faced in getting so far may be read in Mr. Liveing's account. Before our men left the trenches outside Hébuterne they were in a heavy barrage, and the open valley of the No Man's Land hissed, as Mr. Liveing says, like an engine, with machine-gun bullets. Nevertheless, our men reached the third line of enemy trenches and began to secure the ground which they had captured.

During the afternoon the enemy counter-attacked from the south, and, later in the day, from the north as well. Our men had not enough bombs to hold back the attackers, and were gradually driven back, after very severe hand-to-hand fighting in the trenches, to an evil little bend in the front line directly to the south of Gommecourt Cemetery. At about 11 p.m., after sixteen hours of intense and bitter fighting, they were driven back from this point to their own lines.

Mr. Liveing's story is very well told. It is a simple and most vivid account of a modem battle. No better account has been written in England since the war began. I hope that so rare a talent for narrative may be recognised. I hope, too, that Mr. Liveing may soon be able to give us more stories as full of life as this.

JOHN MASEFIELD

- CHAPTER I -

GATHERING FOR ATTACK

T HE ROADS WERE packed with traffic. Column after column of lorries came pounding along, bearing their freight of shells, trench-mortar bombs, wire, stakes, sandbags, pipes, and a thousand other articles essential for the offensive, so that great dumps of explosives and other material arose in the green wayside places. Staff cars and signallers on motor-bikes went busily on their way. Ambulances hurried backwards and forwards between the line and the Casualty Clearing Station, for the days of June were hard days for the infantry who dug the "leaping-off" trenches, and manned them afterwards through rain and raid and bombardment Horse transport and new batteries hurried to their destinations. "Caterpillars" rumbled up, towing the heavier guns. Infantrymen and sappers marched to their tasks round and about the line.

Roads were repaired, telephone wires placed deep in the ground, trees felled for dug-outs and gun emplacements, water-pipes laid up to the trenches ready to be extended across conquered territory, while small-gauge and large-gauge railways seemed to spring to being in the night.

Then came days of terror for the enemy. Slowly our guns broke forth upon them in a tumult of rage. The Germans in retaliation sprayed our nearer batteries with shrapnel, and threw a barrage of whizz-bangs across the little white road leading into the village of Hébuterne. This feeble retaliation was swallowed up and overpowered by the torrent of metal that now poured incessantly into their territory. Shells from the 18-pounders and trench-mortars cut their wire and demoralised their sentries. Guns of all calibres pounded their system of trenches till it looked for all the world like nothing more than a ploughed field. The sky was filled with our aeroplanes wheeling about and directing the work of batteries, and with the black and white bursts of anti-aircraft shells. Shells from the 9.2 howitzers crashed into strong points and gun emplacements and hurled them skywards. Petrol shells licked up the few remaining green-leaved trees in Gommecourt Wood, where observers watched and snipers nested: 15-inch naval guns, under the vigilant guidance of observation balloons, wrought deadly havoc in Bapaume and other villages and billets behind their lines.

Thrice were the enemy enveloped in gas and smoke, and, as they stood-to in expectation of attack, were mown down by a torrent of shells.

The bombardment grew and swelled and brought down showers of rain. Yet the ground remained comparatively dry and columns of dust arose from the roads as hoof and wheel crushed their broken surfaces and battalions of infantry, with songs and jests, marched up to billets and bivouacs just behind the line, ready to give battle.

- CHAPTER II -
EVE OF ATTACK

BOOM! ABSOLUTE SILENCE for a minute. Boom! followed quickly by a more distant report from a fellow-gun. At each bellowing roar from the 9.2 near by, bits of the ceiling clattered on to the floor of the billet and the wall-plaster trickled down on to one's valise, making a sound like soot coming down a chimney.

It was about three o'clock in the morning. I did not look at my watch, as its luminous facings had faded away months before and I did not wish to disturb my companions by lighting a match. A sigh or a groan came from one part of the room or another, showing that our bombardment was troublesome even to the sleepers, and a rasping noise occasionally occurred when W——k, my Company Commander, turned round uneasily on his bed of wood and rabbit-wire.

I plunged farther down into the recesses of my flea-bag, though its linings had broken down and my feet stuck out at the bottom. Then I pulled my British Warm over me and muffled my head and ears in it to escape the regularly-repeated roar of the 9.2. Though the whole house seemed to be shaking to bits at every minute, the noise was muffled to a less ear-splitting fury and I gradually sank into a semi-sleep.

About six o'clock I awoke finally, and after an interval the battery stopped its work. At half-past seven I hauled myself out of my valise and sallied forth into the courtyard, clad in a British Warm, pyjamas, and gum-boots, to make my toilet. I blinked as I came into the light and felt very sleepy. The next moment I was on my hands and knees, with every nerve of my brain working like a mill-stone. A vicious "swish" had sounded over my head, and knowing its meaning I had turned for the nearest door and slipped upon the cobbled stones of the yard. I picked myself up and fled for that door just as the inevitable "crash" came. This happened to be the door to the servants' quarters, and they were vastly amused. We looked out of the window at the *débris* which was rising into the air. Two more "crumps" came whirling over the house, and with shattering explosions lifted more *débris* into the air beyond the farther side of the courtyard. Followed a burst of shrapnel and one more "crump", and the enemy's retaliation on the 9.2 and its crew had ceased. The latter, however, had descended into their dug-out, while the gun remained unscathed. Not so some of our own men.

We were examining the nose-cap of a shell which had hit the wall of our billet, when a corporal came up, who said hurriedly to W——k, "Corporal G——'s been killed and four men wounded."

The whole tragedy had happened so swiftly, and this sudden announcement of the death of one of our best N.C.O.s had come as such a shocks that all we did was to stare at each other with the words:

"My God ! Corporal G—— gone! It's impossible."

One expects shells and death in the line, but three or four miles behind it one grows accustomed, so to speak, to live in a fool's paradise. We went round to see our casualties, and I found two of my platoon, bandaged in the leg and arm, sitting in a group of their pals, who were congratulating them on having got "soft Blighty ones." The Company Quartermaster-Sergeant showed me a helmet, which was lying outside the billet when the shells came over, with a triangular gash in it, into which one could almost place one's fist. At the body of Corporal G—— I could not bring myself to look. The poor fellow had been terribly hit in the back and neck, and, I confess it openly, I had not the courage, and felt that it would be a sacrilege, to gaze on the mangled remains of one whom I had valued so much as an N.C.O. and grown to like so much as a man during the last ten months.

Dark clouds were blowing over in an easterly direction; a cheerless day added to the general gloom. We had a Company Officers' final consultation on the plans for the morrow, after which I held an inspection of my platoon, and gave out some further orders. On my return to the billet W——k told me that the attack had been postponed for two days owing to bad weather. Putting aside all thought of orders for the time being, we issued out rum to the men, indulged in a few "tots" ourselves, and settled down to a pleasant evening.

*   *   *   *   *

In a little courtyard on the evening of June 30 I called the old platoon to attention for the last time, shook hands with the officers left in reserve, marched off into the road, and made up a turning to the left on to the Blue Track. We had done about a quarter of the ground between Bayencourt and Sailly-au-Bois when a messenger hurried up to tell me to halt, as several of the platoons of the L—— S—— had to pass us. We sat down by a large shell-hole, and the men lit up their pipes and cigarettes and shouted jokes to the men of the other regiment as they passed by.

It was a very peaceful evening - remarkably peaceful, now that the guns were at rest. A light breeze played eastward. I sat with my face towards the sunset, wondering a little if this was the last time that I should see it. One often reads of this sensation in second-rate novels. I must say that I had always thought it greatly "overdone"; but a great zest in the splendour of life swept over me as I sat there in the glow of that setting sun, and also a great calmness that gave me heart to do my uttermost on the morrow. My father had enclosed a little card in his last letter to me with the words upon it of the prayer of an old cavalier of the seventeenth century - Sir Jacob Astley - before the battle of Newbury: - "Lord, I shall be very busy this day. I may forget Thee, but do not Thou forget me." A peculiar old prayer, but I kept on repeating it to myself with great comfort that evening. My men were rather quiet. Perhaps the general calmness was affecting them with kindred thoughts, though an Englishman never shows them. On the left stood the stumpy spire of Bazencourt Church just left by us. On the right lay Sailly-au-Bois in its girdle of trees. Along the side of the valley which ran out from behind Sailly-au-Bois, arose numerous lazy pillars of smoke from the wood fires and kitchens of an artillery encampment An English aeroplane, with a swarm of black puffs around it betokening German shells, was gleaming in the setting sun. It purred monotonously, almost drowning the screech of occasional shells which were dropping by a distant château. The calm before the storm sat brooding over everything.

The kilted platoons having gone on their way, we resumed our journey, dipping into the valley behind Sailly-au-Bois, and climbing the farther side, as I passed the officers' mess hut belonging to an anti-aircraft battery, which had taken up a position at the foot of the valley, and whence came a pleasant sound of clinking glass, a wild desire for permanent comfort affected me.

Rounding the outskirts of Sailly-au-Bois, we arrived in the midst of the battery positions nesting by the score in the level plain behind Hébuterne. The batteries soon let us know of their presence. Red flashes broke out in the gathering darkness, followed by quick reports.

To the right one could discern the dim outlines of platoons moving up steadily and at equal distances like ourselves. One could just catch the distant noise of spade clinking on rifle. When I turned my gaze to the front of these troops, I saw yellow-red flashes licking upon the horizon, where our shells were finding their mark. Straight in front, whither we were bound, the girdle of trees round Hébuterne shut out these flashes from view, but by the noise that came from beyond those trees one knew that the German trenches were receiving exactly the same intensity of fire there. Every now and then this belt of trees was being thrown into sharp relief by German star-shells, which rocketed into the sky one after the other like display of fireworks, while at times a burst of hostile shrapnel would throw a weird, red light on the twinkling poplars which surrounded the cemetery.

As we marched on towards the village (I do not mind saying it) I experienced that unpleasant sensation of wondering whether I should be lying out this time tomorrow - stiff and cold in that land beyond the trees, where the red shrapnel burst and the star-shells flickered. I remember hoping that, if the fates so decreed, I should not leave too great a gap in my family, and, best hope of all, that I should instead be speeding home in an ambulance on the road that stretched along to our left. I do not think that I am far wrong when I say that those thoughts were occurring to every man in the silent platoon behind me. Not that we were downhearted. If you had asked the question, you would have been greeted by a cheery "No!" We were all full of determination to do our best next day, but one cannot help enduring rather an unusual "party feeling" before going into an attack.

Suddenly a German shell came screaming towards us. It hurtled overhead and fell behind us with muffled detonation in Sailly-au-Bois. Several more screamed over us as we went along, and it was peculiar to hear the shells of both sides echoing backwards and forwards in the sky at the same time.

We were about four hundred yards from the outskirts of Hébuterne, when I was made aware of the fact that the platoon in front of me had stopped. I immediately stopped my platoon. I sat the men down along a bank, and we waited - a wait which was whiled away by various incidents. I could hear a dog barking, and just see two gunner officers who were walking unconcernedly about the battery positions and whistling for it. The next thing that happened was a red flash in the air about two hundred yards away, and a pinging noise as bits of shrapnel shot into the ground round about. One of my men, S—— (the poor chap was killed next day), called to me: "Look at that fire in Sailly, sir!" I turned round and saw a great yellow flare illuminating the sky in the direction of Sailly, the fiery end of some barn or farm-building, where a high explosive had found its billet.

We remained in this spot for nearly a quarter of an hour, after which R——d's platoon began to move on, and I followed at a good distance with mine. We made our way to the clump of trees over which the shrapnel had burst a few minutes before. Suddenly we found ourselves floundering in a sunken road flooded with water knee-deep. This was not exactly pleasant, especially when my guide informed me that he was not quite certain as to our whereabouts. Luckily, we soon gained dry ground again, turned off into a bit of trench which brought us into the village, and made for the dump by the church, where we were to pick up our materials. When we reached the church - or, rather, its ruins - the road was so filled with parties and platoons, and it was becoming so dark, that it took us some time before we found the dump. Fortunately, the first person whom I spotted was the Regimental Sergeant-Major, and I handed over to him the carrying-party which I had to detail, also despatching the rum and soup parties - the latter to the company cooker.

Leaving the platoon in charge of Sergeant S——l, I went with my guide in search of the dump. In the general *mêlée* I bumped into W——k. We found the rabbit wire, barbed wire, and other material in a shell-broken outhouse, and, grabbing hold of it, handed the stuff out to the platoon.

As we filed through the village the reflections of star-shells threw weird lights on half-ruined houses; an occasional shell screamed overhead, to burst with a dull, echoing sound within the shattered walls of former cottages; and one could hear the rat-tat-tat of machine-guns. These had a nasty habit of spraying the village with indirect fire, and it was, as always, a relief to enter the recesses of Wood Street without having any one hit. This communication trench dipped into the earth at right angles to the "Boulevard" Street. We clattered along the brick-floored trench, whose walls were overhung with the dewy grass and flowers of the orchard - that wonderful orchard whose aroma had survived the horror and desolation of a two years' warfare, and seemed now only to be intensified to a softer fragrance by the night air.

Arriving at the belt of trees and hedge which marked the confines of the orchard, we turned to the right into Cross Street, which cut along behind the belt of trees into Woman Street.

Turning to the left up Woman Street, and leaving the belt of trees behind, we wound into the slightly undulating ground between Hébuterne and Gommecourt Wood. "Crumps" were bursting round about the communication trench, but at a distance, judging by their report, of at least fifty yards. As we were passing Brigade Headquarters' Dug-out, the Brigade-Major appeared and asked me the number of my platoon. "Number 5," I replied; and he answered "Good," with a touch of relief in his voice - for we had been held up for some time on the way, and my platoon was the first or second platoon of the company to get into the line.

It was shortly after this that "crumps" began to burst dangerously near. There was suddenly a blinding flash and terrific report just to our left. We kept on, with heads aching intolerably. Winding round a curve, we came upon the effects of the shells. The sides of the trench had been blown in, while in the middle of the *débris* lay a dead or unconscious man, and farther on a man groaning faintly upon a stretcher. We scrambled over them, passed a few more wounded and stretcher-bearers, and arrived at the Reserve Line.

Captain W——t was standing at the juncture of Woman Street and the Reserve Line, cool and calm as usual. I asked him if New Woman Street was blocked, but there was no need for a reply. A confused noise of groans and stertorous breathing, and of some one sobbing, came to my ears, and above it all, M—— W—— 's voice saying to one of his men: "It's all right, old chap. It's all over now." He told me afterwards that a shell had landed practically in the trench, killing two men in front of him and one behind, and wounding several others, but not touching himself.

It was quite obvious to me that it was impossible to proceed to the support trench via New Woman Street, and at any rate my Company Commander had given me orders to go over the top from the reserve to the support line, so, shells or no shells, and leaving Sergeant S——l to bring up the rear of the platoon, I scaled a ladder leaning on the side of the trench and walked over the open for about two hundred yards. My guide and I jumped into New Woman Street just before it touched the support line, and we were soon joined by several other men of the platoon.

We had already suffered three casualties, and going over the top in the darkness, the men had lost touch. The ration party also had not arrived yet I despatched the guide to bring up the remainder, and proceeded to my destination with about six men. About fifteen yards farther up the trench I found a series of shell-holes threading their way off to the left. By the light of some German star-shells I discerned an officer groping about these holes, and I stumbled over mounds and hollows towards him.

"Is this the support line?" I asked, rather foolishly.

"Yes," he replied, "but there isn't much room in it." I saw that he was an officer of the Royal Engineers.

"I'm putting my smoke-bombers down here," he continued, "but you'll find more room over towards the sunken road."

He showed me along the trench - or the remains of it - and went off to carry out his own plans. I stumbled along till I could just distinguish the outlines of the sunken road. The trench in this direction was blown in level with the ground. I returned to W——k, whose headquarters were at the juncture of New Woman Street and the support line, telling him that the trench by the sunken road was untenable, and that I proposed placing my platoon in a smaller length of trench, and spreading them out fanwise when we started to advance. To this he agreed, and putting his hand on my shoulder in his characteristic fashion, informed me in a whisper that the attack was to start at 7.30 A.M. As far as I can remember it was about one o'clock by now, and more of my men had come up. I ensconced them by sections. No. 1 section on the left and No. 4 on the right in shell-holes and the remains of the trench along a distance of about forty yards, roughly half the length of the trench that they were to have occupied. At the same time I gave orders to my right- and left-hand guides to incline off to the right and left respectively when the advance started. I was walking back to my headquarters, a bit of trench behind a traverse, when a German searchlight, operating from the direction of Serre Wood, turned itself almost dead on me. I was in my trench in a second.

Shortly afterwards Sergeant S——r arrived with No. 8 platoon. I showed him one or two available portions of trench, but most of his men had to crowd in with mine. The Lewis-gunners, who arrived last, found only a ruined bit of trench next to my "headquarters," while they deposited their guns and equipment in a shell-hole behind.

It was somewhere about four or half-past when I made my last inspection. I clambered over the back of the trench and stood still for a moment or so. Everything was uncannily silent There was just a suspicion of whiteness creeping into the sky beyond the rising ground opposite. Over towards the left rose the remains of Gommecourt Wood. Half its trees had gone since the last time that I had seen it, and the few that remained stood, looking like so many masts in a harbour, gaunt and charred by our petrol shells.

The men in the left fire-bay seemed quite comfortable. But, standing and looking down the trench, it suddenly dawned upon me that I was gazing right into a line of chalky German trenches, and consequently that the enemy in those trenches could look straight into this trench. I left instructions with the corporal in charge of that section to build up a barricade in the gap before daybreak. As I went along the rest of our frontage, Sergeant S——l doled out the rum.

I retired to my "headquarters," but not so Sergeant S——l, who seemed not to bother a bit about the increasing light and the bullets which came phitting into the ground in rather an unpleasant quantity. I was glad when I had finally got him down into the trench. W——k had also told him to get in, for he remarked —

"Captain W——k, 'e says to me, 'Get into the trench, S——l, you b—— fool!' so I've got in."

He was just in time. A prelude of shrapnel screamed along, bursting over-head, and there followed an hour's nerve-racking bombardment.

(Above) British infantry assemble for the 'Big Push'. Here we see a company of the Public Schools Battalion at 'White City' near Beaumont Hamel, prior to the Battle of the Somme.

(Below) The German infantry on the Somme were a mixture of regular formations and reserve formations. These men are from Landwehr Infantry Regiment Nr. 1.

*(Above) A historic meeting in France just prior to the battle.
(From left to right) Sir Henry Rawlinson, Sir Douglas Haig, and King George.*

(Below) A British camp on the eve of the great offensive. The dusty roads were alive with movement and, in the foreground, the men can be seen collecting their equipment for the coming ordeal.

(Above) *The barrage which preceded the Battle of the Somme began on 24ᵗʰ June. In the week that followed 1,732,873 shells were fired by British guns along the 14 mile front.*

(Below) *An Allied 9.2-inch gun mounted on a specially designed railway wagon fires on German positions during the preliminary bombardment.*

(Above) Nerve-racking work: A heavy British howitzer on a rail emplacement bombarding the German positions, in hope of laying the foundations for the success of the large-scale infantry attack to follow.

(Below) An eight-inch Mark V howitzer in a camouflaged emplacement, near Carnoy, July, 1916.

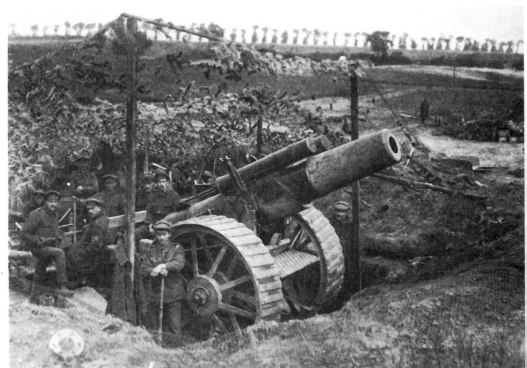

(Above) Men of the R.A.O.C. playing cards on a dump of trench mortar ammunition known to British troops as 'Toffee Apples'. This photograph was taken at Acheux in July, 1916.

(Below) A crew operates their 8-inch howitzer in a heavy rain storm. The offensive had to be postponed due to persistent rain.

(Above) A British ammunition convoy on a road near Albert, July, 1916.

(Below) The British howitzers continue to pound the German trenches in the build up to the 'Big Push'.

(Above) The scale of the bombardment can be gauged from this remarkable photograph of empty shell cases, piled high in this dump at Fricourt, September, 1916.

(Below) Captured German trenches, La Boiselle, July, 1916. The true nature of the barbed wire entanglements can be understood from this excellent study.

The steps leading down to a huge underground German shelter at Bernafay Wood, near Montauban.
This photograph gives a clear idea of the size and depth of many German dug-outs on the Somme.

(Above) A German trench at Ovillers after bombardment by the British artillery. Ovillers was the scene of some of the fiercest fighting at the beginning of the great advance in July, 1916.

(Below) German infantry in a shelter wait anxiously for the British bombardment to end. The strength and depth of the German dug-outs proved to be the equal of the British bombardment.

(Above) Barbed wire at Beaumont Hamel, July, 1916. The impenetrable nature of this type of defence is clear from this photograph.

(Below) The village of Beaumont Hamel after its capture during the Battle of the Somme. So intense was the bombardment that the village was reduced to brick dust.

(Above) Various types of warning bells and rattles were used during the battle. This gas sentry is wearing an early form of gas hood impregnated with hyposulphate of soda and phenate to protect the wearer.

(Below) This photograph shows the men of the Lancashire Fusiliers being addressed by their divisional commander on the eve of the great battle.

(Above) The scene in a communication trench in the build up to the opening phase of the offensive which later became known as the Battle of Albert, July, 1916.

(Below) A battalion of the London Scottish marching to the trenches on the Somme.

(Above) The offensive was meticulously planned, here a Brigadier General and two Staff Officers are studying a map in Mametz Wood, July, 1916.

(Below) In preparation for the assault on Beaumont Hamel, on the morning of 1st July, 1916, the 1st Battalion Lancashire Fusiliers fix their bayonets.

(Above) More men of the 1ˢᵗ Battalion Lancashire Fusiliers fix bayonets in readiness for an attack on the Somme. Many of these men would become casualties shortly after this photograph was taken.

(Below) During the early stages of the battle a communication trench is used for a well-earned rest by a ration party of the Royal Irish Rifles.

The 4ᵗʰ Battalion, the Worcester Regiment (29ᵗʰ Division), resting on their way to the trenches. The strange devices attached to their rifles are wire-cutters which proved to be ineffective.

(Above) Reserve troops armed with rifles, mortars and Lewis guns await the order to attack near Ginchy.

(Below) Men of the Warwickshire Regiment resting near Jacob's Ladder, Beaumont Hamel, July, 1916.

- CHAPTER III -

ATTACK

DAWN WAS BREAKING. The morning was cool after a chill night - a night of waiting in blown-down trenches with not an inch to move to right or left, of listening to the enemy's shells as they left the guns and came tearing and shrieking towards you, knowing all the time that they were aimed for your particular bit of trench and would land in it or by it, of awaiting that sudden, ominous silence, and then the crash - perhaps death.

I, for my part, had spent most of the night sitting on a petrol tin, wedged between the two sides of the trench and two human beings - my sergeant on the left and a corporal on the right. Like others, I had slept for part of the time despite the noise and danger, awakened now and then by the shattering crash of a shell or the hopeless cry for stretcher-bearers.

But morning was coming at last, and the bombardment had ceased. The wind blew east, and a few fleecy clouds raced along the blue sky overhead. The sun was infusing more warmth into the air. There was the freshness and splendour of a summer morning over everything. In fact, as one man said, it felt more as if we were going to start off for a picnic than for a battle.

"Pass it down to Sergeant H—— that Sergeant S——1 wishes him the top o' the mornin'," said my sergeant But Sergeant H——, who was in charge of the company's Lewis-guns, and had been stationed in the next fire-trench, was at present groping his way to safety with a lump of shrapnel in his back.

An occasional shell sang one way or the other. Otherwise all was quiet. We passed down the remains of the rum.

Sergeant S——1 pressed me to take some out of a mess-tin lid. I drank a very little - the first and last "tot" I took during the battle. It warmed me up. Some time after this I looked at my watch and found it was a minute or two before 6.25 A.M. I turned to the corporal, saying -

"They'll just about start now."

The words were not out of my mouth before the noise, which had increased a trifle during the last twenty minutes, suddenly swelled into a gigantic roar. Our guns had started. The din was so deafening that one could not hear the crash of German shells exploding in our own lines.

Sergeant S——1 was standing straight up in the trench and looking over to see the effects of our shells. It was a brave thing to do, but absolutely reckless. I pulled him down by the tail of his tunic. He got up time and again, swearing that he would "take on the whole b—— German army." He gave us pleasing information of the effects of our bombardment, but as I did not want him to lose his life prematurely, I saw to it that we kept him down in the trench till the time came for a display of bravery, in which he was not lacking.

We had been told that the final bombardment that day would be the most intense one since the beginning of the war. The attack was to encircle what was almost generally considered the strongest German "fortress" on the Western Front, the stronghold of Gommecourt Wood. There was need of it, therefore.

Just over the trenches, almost raising the hair on one's head (we were helmeted, I must say, but that was the feeling), swished the smaller shells from the French .75 and English 18-pounder batteries. They gave one the sensation of being under a swiftly rushing stream. The larger shells kept up a continuous shrieking overhead, falling on the enemy's trenches with the roar of a cataract, while every now and then a noise as of thunder sounded above all when our trench-mortar shells fell amongst the German wire, blowing it to bits, making holes like mine craters, and throwing dirt and even bits of metal into our own trenches.

I have often tried to call to memory the intellectual, mental and nervous activity through which I passed during that hour of hellish bombardment and counter-bombardment, that last hour before we leapt out of our trenches into No Man's Land. I give the vague recollection of that ordeal for what it is worth. I had an excessive desire for the time to come when I could go "over the top," when I should be free at last from the noise of the bombardment, free from the prison of my trench, free to walk across that patch of No Man's Land and opposing trenches till I got to my objective, or, if I did not go that far, to have my fate decided for better or for worse. I experienced, too, moments of intense fear during close bombardment. I felt that if I was blown up it would be the end of all things so far as I was concerned. The idea of after-life seemed ridiculous in the presence of such frightful destructive force. Again the prayer of that old cavalier kept coming to my mind. At any rate, one could but do one's best, and I hoped that a higher power than all that which was around would not overlook me or any other fellows on that day. At one time, not very long before the moment of attack, I felt to its intensest depth the truth of the proverb, "Carpe diem." What was time? I had another twenty minutes in which to live in comparative safety. What was the difference between twenty minutes and twenty years? Really and truly what was the difference? I was living at present, and that was enough. I am afraid that this working of mind will appear unintelligible, I cannot explain it further. I think that others who have waited to "go over" will realise its meaning. Above all, perhaps, and except when shells falling near by brought one back to reality, the intense cascade-like noise of our own shells rushing overhead numbed for the most part of the time one's nervous and mental system. Listening to this pandemonium, one felt like one of an audience at a theatre and not in the least as if one was in any way associated with it oneself.

Still, the activity of a man's nerves, though dulled to a great extent inwardly, were bound to show externally. I turned to the corporal. He was a brave fellow, and had gone through the Gallipoli campaign, but he was shaking all over, and white as parchment. I expect that I was just the same.

"We must be giving them hell," I said. "I don't think they're sending much back."

"I don't think much, sir," he replied.

I hardly think we believed each other. Looking up out of the trench beyond him, I saw huge, black columns of smoke and *débris* rising up from our communication trench. Then, suddenly, there was a blinding "crash" just by us. We were covered in mud which flopped out of the trench, and the evil-smelling fumes of lyddite. The cry for stretcher-bearers was passed hurriedly up the line again.

Followed "crash" after "crash," and the pinging of shrapnel which flicked into the top of the trench, the purring noise of flying nose-caps and soft thudding sounds as they fell into the parapet.

It was difficult to hear one another talking. Sergeant S——1 was still full of the "get at 'em" spirit. So were we all. The men were behaving splendidly. I passed along the word to "Fix swords."

We could not see properly over the top of the trench, but smoke was going over. The attack was about to begin - it was beginning. I passed word round the comer of the traverse, asking whether they could see if the second wave was starting. It was just past 7.30 a.m.. The third wave, of which my platoon formed a part, was due to start at 7.30 plus 45 seconds - at the same time as the second wave in my part of the line. The corporal got up, so I realised that the second wave was assembling on the top to go over. The ladders had been smashed or used as stretchers long ago. Scrambling out of a battered part of the trench, I arrived on top, looked down my line of men, swung my rifle forward as a signal, and started off at the prearranged walk.

A continuous hissing noise all around one, like a railway engine letting off steam, signified that the German machine-gunners had become aware of our advance. I nearly trod on a motionless form. It lay in a natural position, but the ashen face and fixed, fearful eyes told me that the man had just fallen. I did not recognise him then. I remember him now. He was one of my own platoon.

To go back for a minute. The scene that met my eyes as I stood on the parapet of our trench for that one second is almost indescribable. Just in front the ground was pitted by innumerable shell-holes. More holes opened suddenly every now and then. Here and there a few bodies lay about. Farther away, before our front line and in No Man's Land, lay more. In the smoke one could distinguish the second line advancing. One man after another fell down in a seemingly natural manner, and the wave melted away. In the background, where ran the remains of the German lines and wire, there was a mass of smoke, the red of the shrapnel bursting amid it. Amongst it, I saw Captain H—— and his men attempting to enter the German front line. The Boches had met them on the parapet with bombs. The whole scene reminded me of battle pictures, at which in earlier years I had gazed with much amazement. Only this scene, though it did not seem more real, was infinitely more terrible. Everything stood still for a second, as a panorama painted with three colours - the white of the smoke, the red of the shrapnel and blood, the green of the grass.

If I had felt nervous before, I did not feel so now, or at any rate not in anything like the same degree. As I advanced, I felt as if I was in a dream, but I had all my wits about me. We had been told to walk. Our boys, however, rushed forward with splendid impetuosity to help their comrades and smash the German resistance in the front line. What happened to our materials for blocking the German communication trench, when we got to our objective, I should not like to think. I kept up a fast walking pace and tried to keep the line together. This was impossible. When we had jumped clear of the remains of our front line trench, my platoon slowly disappeared through the line stretching out. For a long time, however, Sergeant S——1, Lance-corporal M——, Rifleman D——, whom I remember being just in front of me, raising his hand in the air and cheering, and myself kept together. Eventually Lance-corporal M—— was the only one of my platoon left near me, and I shouted out to him, "Let's try and keep together." It was not long, however, before we also parted company. One thing I remember very well about this time, and that was that a hare jumped up and rushed towards and past me through the dry, yellowish grass, its eyes bulging with fear.

We were dropping into a slight valley. The shell-holes were less few, but bodies lay all over the ground, and a terrible groaning arose from all sides. At one time we seemed to be advancing in little groups. I was at the head of one for a moment or two, only to realise shortly afterwards that I was alone.

I came up to the German wire. Here one could hear men shouting to one another and the wounded groaning above the explosions of shells and bombs and the rattle of machine-guns. I found myself with J——, an officer of "C" company, afterwards killed while charging a machine-gun in the open. We looked round to see what our fourth line was doing. My company's fourth line had no leader. Captain W——k, wounded twice, had fallen into a shell-hole, while Sergeant S——r had been killed during the preliminary bombardment. Men were kneeling and firing. I started back to see if I could bring them up, but they were too far away. I made a cup of my mouth and shouted, as J—— was shouting. We could not be heard. I turned round again and advanced to a gap in the German wire. There was a pile of our wounded here on the German parapet.

Suddenly I cursed. I had been scalded in the left hip. A shell, I thought, had blown up in a water-logged crump-hole and sprayed me with boiling water. Letting go of my rifle, I dropped forward full length on the ground. My hip began to smart unpleasantly, and I left a curious warmth stealing down my left leg. I thought it was the boiling water that had scalded me. Certainly my breeches looked as if they were saturated with water. I did not know that they were saturated with blood.

So I lay, waiting with the thought that I might recover my strength (I could barely move) and try to crawl back. There was the greater possibility of death, but there was also the possibility of life. I looked around to see what was happening. In front lay some wounded; on either side of them stakes and shreds of barbed wire twisted into weird contortions by the explosions of our trench-mortar bombs. Beyond this nothing but smoke, interspersed with the red of bursting bombs and shrapnel.

From out this ghastly chaos crawled a familiar figure. It was that of Sergeant K——, bleeding from a wound in the chest. He came crawling towards me.

"Hallo, K——," I shouted.

"Are you hit, sir?" he asked.

"Yes, old chap, I am," I replied.

"You had better try and crawl back," he suggested.

"I don't think I can move," I said.

"I'll take off your equipment for you."

He proceeded very gallantly to do this. I could not get to a kneeling position myself, and he had to get hold of me, and bring me to a kneeling position, before undoing my belt and shoulder-straps. We turned round and started crawling back together. I crawled very slowly at first. Little holes opened in the ground on either side of me, and I understood that I was under the fire of a machine-gun. In front bullets were hitting the turf and throwing it four or five feet into the air. Slowly but steadily I crawled on. Sergeant K—— and I lost sight of one another. I think that he crawled off to the right and I to the left of a mass of barbed wire entanglements.

I was now confronted by a danger from our own side. I saw a row of several men kneeling on the ground and firing. It is probable that they were trying to pick off German machine-gunners, but it seemed very much as if they would "pot" a few of the returning wounded into the bargain.

"For God's sake, stop firing," I shouted.

Words were of no avail. I crawled through them. At last I got on my feet and stumbled blindly along.

I fell down into a sunken road with several other wounded, and crawled up over the bank on the other side. The Germans had a machine-gun on that road, and only a few of us got across. Someone faintly called my name behind me. Looking round, I thought I recognised a man of "C" company. Only a few days later did it come home to me that he was my platoon observer. I had told him to stay with me whatever happened. He had carried out his orders much more faithfully than I had ever meant, for he had come to my assistance, wounded twice in the head himself. He hastened forward to me, but, as I looked round waiting, uncertain quite as to who he was, his rifle clattered on to the ground, and he crumpled up and fell motionless just behind me. I felt that there was nothing to be done for him. He died a hero, just as he had always been in the trenches, full of self-control, never complaining, a ready volunteer. Shortly afterwards I sighted the remains of our front line trench and fell into them.

At first I could not make certain as to my whereabouts. Coupled with the fact that my notions in general were becoming somewhat hazy, the trenches themselves were entirely unrecognisable. They were filled with earth, and about half their original depth. I decided, with that quick, almost semi-conscious intuition that comes to one in moments of peril, to proceed to the left (to one coming from the German lines). As I crawled through holes and over mounds I could hear the vicious spitting of machine-gun bullets. They seemed to skim just over my helmet. The trench, opening out a little, began to assume its old outline. I had reached the head of New Woman Street, though at the time I did not know what communication trench it was - or trouble, for that matter.

The scene at the head of that communication trench is stamped in a blurred but unforgettable way on my mind. In the remains of a wrecked dug-out or emplacement a signaller sat, calmly transmitting messages to Battalion Headquarters. A few bombers were walking along the continuation of the front line. I could distinguish the red grenades on their arms through the smoke. There were more of them at the head of the communication trench. Shells were coming over and blowing up round about.

I asked one of the bombers to see what was wrong with my hip. He started to get out my iodine tube and field dressing. The iodine tube was smashed. I remembered that I had a second one, and we managed to get that out after some time. Shells were coming over so incessantly and close that the bomber advised that we should walk farther down the trench before commencing operations. This done, he opened my breeches and disclosed a small hole in the front of the left hip. It was bleeding fairly freely. He poured in the iodine, and put the bandage round in the best manner possible. We set off down the communication trench again, in company with several bombers, I holding the bandage to my wound. We scrambled up mounds and jumped over craters (rather a painful performance for one wounded in the leg); we halted at times in almost open places, when machine-gun bullets swept unpleasantly near, and one felt the wind of shells as they passed just over, blowing up a few yards away. In my last stages across No Man's Land my chief thought had been, "I must get home now for the sake of my people." Now, for I still remember it distinctly, my thought was, "Will my name appear in the casualty list under the head of 'Boiled' or 'Wounded'?" and I summoned up a mental picture of the two alternatives in black type.

After many escapes we reached the Reserve Line, where a military policeman stood at the head of Woman Street. He held up the men in front of me and directed them to different places. Some one told him that a wounded officer was following. This was, perhaps, as well, for I was an indistinguishable mass of filth and gore. My helmet was covered with mud, my tunic was cut about with shrapnel and bullets and saturated with blood; my breeches had changed from a khaki to a purple hue; my puttees were in tatters; my boots looked like a pair of very muddy clogs.

The military policeman consigned me to the care of some excellent fellow, of what regiment I cannot remember. After walking, or rather stumbling, a short way down Woman Street, my guide and I came upon a gunner Colonel standing outside his dug-out and trying to watch the progress of the battle through his field-glasses.

"Good-morning," he said.

"Good-morning, sir," I replied.

This opening of our little conversation was not meant to be in the least ironical, I can assure you. It seemed quite natural at the time.

"Where are you hit?" he asked.

"In the thigh, sir. I don't think it's anything very bad."

"Good. How are we getting on?"

"Well, I really can't say much for certain, sir. But I got nearly to their front line."

Walking was now becoming exceedingly painful and we proceeded slowly. I choked the groans that would rise to my lips and felt a cold perspiration pouring freely from my face. It was easier to get along by taking hold of the sides of the trench with my hands than by being supported by my guide. A party of bombers or carriers of some description passed us. We stood on one side to let them go by. In those few seconds my wound became decidedly stiffer, and I wondered if I would ever reach the end of the trenches on foot. At length the communication trench passed through a belt of trees, and we found ourselves in Cross Street.

Here was a First Aid Post, and R.A.M.C. men were hard at work. I had known those trenches for a month past, and I had never thought that Cross Street could appear so homelike. Hardly a shell was falling and the immediate din of battle had subsided. The sun was becoming hot, but the trees threw refreshing shadows over the wide, shallow brick-floored trenches built by the French two years before. The R.A.M.C. orderlies were speaking pleasant words, and men not too badly wounded were chatting gaily. I noticed a dresser at work on a man near by, and was pleased to find that the man whose wounds were being attended to was my servant L——. His wound was in the hip, a nasty hole drilled by a machine-gun bullet at close quarters. He showed me his water-bottle, penetrated by another bullet, which had inflicted a further, but slight, wound.

There were many more serious cases than mine to be attended to. After about five or ten minutes an orderly slit up my breeches.

"The wound's in the front of the hip," I said.

"Yes, but there's a larger wound where the bullets come out, sir."

I looked and saw a gaping hole two inches in diameter.

"I think that's a Blighty one, isn't it?" I remarked.

"I should just think so, sir!" he replied.

"Thank God! At last!" I murmured vehemently, conjuring up visions of the good old homeland.

The orderly painted the iodine round both wounds and put on a larger bandage. At this moment R——, an officer of "D" company, came limping into Cross Street.

"Hallo, L——," he exclaimed, "we had better try and get down to hospital together."

We started in a cavalcade to walk down the remaining trenches into the village, not before my servant, who had insisted on staying with me, had remarked -

"I think I should like to go up again now, sir," and to which proposal I had answered very emphatically -

"You won't do anything of the sort, my friend!"

R—— led the way, with a man to help him, next came my servant, then two orderlies carrying a stretcher with a terribly wounded Scottish private on it; another orderly and myself brought up the rear - and a very slow one at that!

Turning a comer, we found ourselves amidst troops of the battalion in reserve to us, all of them eager for news. A subaltern, with whom I had been at a Divisional School, asked how far we had got. I told him that we were probably in their second line by now. This statement caused disappointment. Every one appeared to believe that we had taken the three lines in about ten minutes. I must confess that the night before the attack I had entertained hopes that it would not take us much longer than this. As a matter of fact my battalion, or the remains of it, after three hours of splendid and severe fighting, managed to penetrate into the third line trench.

Loss of blood was beginning to tell, and my progress was getting slower every minute. Each man, as I passed, put his arm forward to help me along and said a cheery word of some kind or other. Down the wide, brick-floored trench we went, past shattered trees and battered cottages, through the rank grass and luxuriant wild flowers, through the rich, unwarlike aroma of the orchard, till we emerged into the village "boulevard."

The orderly held me under the arms till I was put on a wheeled stretcher and hurried along, past the "boulevard pool" with its surrounding elms and willows, and, at the end of the "boulevard," up a street to the left. A short way up this street on the right stood the Advanced Dressing Station - a well-sandbagged house reached through the usual archway and courtyard. A dug-out, supplied with electric light and with an entrance of remarkable sandbag construction, had been tunnelled out beneath the courtyard. This was being used for operations.

In front of the archway and in the road stood two "padrés" directing the continuous flow of stretchers and walking wounded. They appeared to be doing all the work of organisation, while the R.A.M.C. doctors and surgeons had their hands full with dressings and operations. These were the kind of directions:

"Wounded Sergeant? Right. Abdominal wound? All right. Lift him off - gently now. Take him through the arch-way into the dug-out."

"Dead? Yes! Poor fellow, take him down to the Cemetery."

"German? Dug-out No. 2, at the end of the road on the right."

Under the superintendence of the R.C. "padré," a man whose sympathy and kindness I shall never forget, my stretcher was lifted off the carrier and I was placed in the archway. The "padré" loosened my bandage and looked at the wound, when he drew in his breath and asked if I was in much pain.

"Not ail enormous amount," I answered, but asked for something to drink.

"Are you quite sure it hasn't touched the stomach?" he questioned, looking shrewdly at me.

I emphatically denied that it had, and he brought a blood-stained mug with a little tea at the bottom of it. I can honestly say that I never enjoyed a drink so much as that one.

Shells, high explosives and shrapnel, were coming over every now and then. I kept my helmet well over my head. This also served as a shade from the sun, for it was now about ten o'clock and a sultry day. I was able to obtain a view of events round about fairly easily. From time to time orderlies tramped through the archway, bearing stretcher-cases to the dug-out. Another officer had been brought in and placed on the opposite side of the archway. The poor fellow, about nineteen, was more or less unconscious. His head and both hands were covered in bandages crimson with blood. So coated was he with mud and gore that I did not at first recognise him as an officer. At the farther end of the arch a young private of about eighteen was lying on his side, groaning in the agony of a stomach wound and crying "Mother." The sympathetic "padré" did the best he could to comfort him. Out in the road the R.A.M.C. were dressing and bandaging the ever-increasing flow of wounded. Amongst them a captive German R.A.M.C. man, in green uniform, with a Red Cross round his sleeve, was visible, hard at work. Everything seemed so different from the deadly strife a thousand or so yards away. There, foe was inflicting wounds on foe; here were our men attending to the German wounded and the Germans attending to ours. Both sides were working so hard now to save life. There was a human touch about that scene in the ruined Tillage street which filled one with a sense of mingled sadness and pleasure. Here were both sides united in a common attempt to repair the ravages of war. Humanity had at last asserted itself.

It was about eleven o'clock, I suppose, when the "padré" came up again to my stretcher and asked me if I should like to get on, as there was a berth vacant in an ambulance. The stretcher was hoisted up and slid into the bottom berth of the car. The berth above was occupied by an unconscious man. On the other side of the ambulance were four sitting cases - a private, a sergeant, a corporal, and a rifleman, the last almost unconscious. Those of us who could talk were very pleased with life, and I remember saying: "Thank God, we're out of that hell, boys!"

"What's wrong with him?" I asked the corporal, signifying the unconscious man.

"Hit in the lungs, sir. They've set him up on purpose."

The corporal, pulling out his cigarette case, offered cigarettes all round, and we started to smoke. The last scene that I saw in Hébuterne was that of three men dressing a tall badly wounded Prussian officer lying on the side of the road. The ambulance turned the corner out of the village. There followed three "crashes" and dust flew on to the floor of the car.

"Whizz-bangs," was the corporal's laconical remark.

We had passed the German road barrage, and were on our way to peace and safety.

- CHAPTER IV -

TOLL OF ATTACK

WE CLIMBED THE little white road which led through the battery positions now almost silent, topped the crest, and dipped into Sailly-au-Bois. The village had been very little shelled since the night before, and appeared the same as ever, except that the intense traffic, which had flowed into it for the past month, had ceased. Limbers and lorries had done their work, and the only objects which filled the shell-scarred streets were slow-moving ambulances, little blood-stained groups of "walking wounded," and the troops of a new division moving up into the line.

Though we were all in some pain as the ambulance jolted along through the ruts in the side of the road, we felt rather sorry for those poor chaps as they peered inside the car. Our fate was decided, theirs still hung in the balance. How often on the march one had looked back oneself into a passing ambulance and wished, rather shamefully, for a "Blighty" one. Sun-burnt and healthy they looked as they shouted after us: "Good luck, boys, give our love to Blighty."

At the end of the village the ambulance swung off on a road leading to the left. It must have crossed the track by which my platoon and I had gone up the night before. About 11.30 A.M. we arrived at Couin, the headquarters of the First Field Ambulance.

A hum of conversation and joking arose from every side, and, with some exceptions, you could not have found such a cheery gathering anywhere. The immediate strain of battle had passed, and friends meeting friends compared notes of their experiences in the "show." Here a man with a bandaged arm was talking affectionately to a less fortunate "pal" on a stretcher, and asking him if he could do anything for him; it is extraordinary how suffering knits men together, and how much sympathy is brought out in a man at the sight of a badly wounded comrade: yonder by the huts an orderly assisted a "walking case," shot through the lungs and vomiting blood freely.

Near by I recognised E——'s servant of the L—— S——. When he had finished giving some tea or water to a friend, I hailed him and asked him if Mr. E—— was hit. Mr. E——, he told me, had been laid up for some days past, and had not taken part in the attack. He was, however, going round and writing letters for the men. Would I like to see him? We were fairly good acquaintances, so I said that I should. Presently he arrived.

"Bad luck, old chap. Where have you caught it?" he asked.

"In the thigh," I replied.

He wrote two post-cards home for me, one home and another to relatives, and I did my best to sign them. I remember that on one of them was inscribed: "This is to let you know that E—— has been caught bending," and wondering what my grandfather, a doctor, would make out of that!

The sun was beating down on us now, and since, after I had been duly labelled "G.S.W. (gun-shot wound) Back," a Medical Staff Officer advised that I should be transferred into the officers' hut, I entered its cooler shades with much gladness.

Captain W——t came in soon afterwards. In the second line German trench he had looked over the parados to see if any opposition was coming up from the third line trench, and had been hit by a machine-gun bullet in the shoulder. In making his way home he had been hit twice again in the shoulder. H—— also put in an appearance with a bullet wound in the arm. He had taken a party of "walking wounded" up to Sailly-au-Bois, and got a car on. A doctor brought round the familiar old beverage of tea, which in large quantities, and in company with whisky, had helped us through many an unpleasant day in the trenches. Captain W——t refused it, and insisted on having some bread and jam. I took both with much relish, and, having appeased an unusually large appetite, got an orderly to wash my face and hands, which were coated with blood.

"I dare say you feel as you was gettin' back to civilisation again, sir," he said. Much refreshed, and quietly looking at a new number of *The Tatler*, I certainly felt as if I was, though, in spite of an air ring, the wound was feeling rather uncomfortable. At the end of the hut two or three poor fellows were dying of stomach wounds. It was a peculiar contrast to hear two or three men chatting gaily just outside my end of the hut, I could only catch fragments of the conversation, which I give here.

"When Mr. A—— gave the order to advance, I went over like a bird."

"The effect of the rum, laddie!"

"Mr A—— was going strong too."

"What's happened to Mr. A——, do you know?"

"Don't know. I didn't see 'im after that."

"'E's all right. Saw him just now. Got a wound in the arm."

"Good, Isn't the sun fine here? Couldn't want a better morning for an attack, could you?"

The hut was filling rapidly, and the three stomach eases being quite hopeless were removed outside. A doctor brought in an officer of the K——'s. He was quite dazed, and sank full length on a bed, passing his hand across his face and moaning. He was not wounded, but had been blown up whilst engaged in cutting a communication trench across No Man's Land, they told me. It was not long, however, before he recovered his senses sufficiently enough to walk with help to an ambulance. A "padré" entered, supporting a young officer of the ——, a far worse case of shell shock, and laid him out on the bed. He had no control over himself, and was weeping hysterically.

"For God's sake don't let me go back, don't send me back!" he cried.

The "padré" tried to comfort him.

"You'll soon be in a nice hospital at the Base, old chap, or probably in England."

He looked at the "padré" blankly, not understanding a word that he was saying.

A more extraordinary case of shell shock was that of an officer lying about three beds down from me. In the usual course of events an R.A.M.C. corporal asked him his name.

"F——," he replied in a vague tone.

The corporal thought that he had better make certain, so with as polite a manner as possible looked at his identification disc.

"It puts Lt. B—— here," he said.

There followed a lengthy argument, at the end of which the patient said ——

"Well, it's no use. You had better give it up. I don't know what my name is!"

A Fusilier officer was carried in on a stretcher and laid next to me. After a time he said ——

"Is your name L——?"

I replied affirmatively.

"Don't you recognise me?" he questioned.

I looked at him, but could not think where I had seen him before.

"My name's D——. I was your Company Quartermaster-Sergeant in the Second Battalion." Then I remembered him, though it had been hard to recognise him in officer's uniform, blood-stained and tattered at that. We compared notes of our experiences since I had left the second line of my battalion in England nearly a year before, until, soon afterwards, he was taken out to an ambulance.

At the other end of the hut it was just possible to see an officer tossing to and fro deliriously on a stretcher. I use the word "deliriously" though he was probably another case of shell shock. He was wounded also, judging by the bandages which swathed the middle part of his body. The poor fellow thought that he was still fighting, and every now and again broke out like this——

"Keep 'em off, boys. Keep 'em off. Give me a bomb, sergeant. Get down! My God! I'm hit. Put some more of those sandbags on the barricade. These damned shells! Can I stand it any longer? Come on, boys. Come along, sergeant! We must go for them. Oh! My God! I must stick it!"

After a time the cries became fainter, and the stretcher was taken out.

About three o'clock I managed to get a doctor to inject me with anti-tetanus. I confess that I was rather anxious about getting this done, for in crawling back across No Man's Land my wound had been covered with mud and dirt. The orderly, who put on the iodine, told me that the German artillery was sending shrapnel over the ridge. This was rather disconcerting, but, accustomed as I had become to shrapnel at close quarters, the sounds seemed so distant that I did not bother more about them.

It must have been about four o'clock when my stretcher was picked up and I passed once again into the warm sunlight. Outside an orderly relieved me of my steel and gas helmets, in much the same way as the collector takes your ticket when you pass through the gates of a London terminus in a taxi Once more the stretcher was slid into an ambulance, and I found myself in company with a young subaltern of the K——'s. He was very cheery, and continued to assert that we should all be in "Blighty" in a day or two's time. When the A.S.C. driver appeared at the entrance of the car and confirmed our friend's opinion, I began to entertain the most glorious visions of the morrow - visions which I need hardly say did not come true.

"How were you hit?" I asked the officer of the K——'s.

"I got a machine-gun bullet in the pit of the stomach while digging that communication trench into No Man's Land. It's been pretty bad, but the paints going now, and I think I shall be all right."

Then he recognised the man on the stretcher above me.

"Hullo, laddie," he said. "What have they done to you?"

"I've been hit in the left wrist and the leg, sir. I hope you aren't very bad."

The engine started, and we set off on our journey to the Casualty Clearing Station. For the last time we passed the villages, which we had come to know so intimately in the past two months during rest from the trenches. There was Souastre, where one had spent pleasant evenings at the Divisional Theatre; St. Amand with its open square in front of the church, the meeting-place of the villagers, now deserted save for two or three soldiers; Gaudiempré, the headquarters of an Army

(Above) A German trench captured by British troops near the Albert-Bapaume road at Ovillers-la-Boiselle, July, 1916. The men are from A Company, 11th Battalion, the Cheshire Regiment.

(Below) The Battle of Albert begins with the explosion of the mine near Beaumont Hamel, 1st July, 1916. The explosion was filmed by Geoffrey Malins and appears in the famous Somme documentary.

(Above) The hour has struck! A good contemporary visualisation of the British first line of attack taking up position in front of their barbed-wire defences, 1st July, 1916.

(Below) The Battle of the Somme gets underway, a contemporary illustration of the attack by the Ulster Division on the 1st July, 1916.

(Above) The attack upon German trenches by British troops, 1st July, 1916. The figures of the advancing men can be clearly seen against the white of the trenches, excavated from the chalk soil.

(Below) With the British barrage and German counter-barrage on the left, an artist is able to depict the attack of the British infantry on the Schwaben Redoubt.

(Above) At the outset of the 'Big Push': This contemporary illustration depicts British troops advancing over the captured German trenches on the Somme, 1st July, 1916.

(Below) An impressive photographic record of troops going over the top during the Battle of the Somme.

(Above) Pushing through the wire near Thièpval, men of the Wiltshire Regiment attack, August, 1916.

(Below) In a contemporary illustration entitled 'Their Last Hope', demoralised German soldiers are shown imploring clemency from advancing British troops.

(*Above*) *A British soldier puts his Lewis light machine-gun in to action near Ovillers, July, 1916.*

(*Below*) *This image of an officer leading his under heavy shell fire has become one of the most enduring images from the Battle of the Somme.*

(Above) The London Territorials storm Pozières during the latter stages of the Battle of the Somme.

(Below) The German Stahlhelm or 'steel helmet' was first introduced during the Battle of Verdun in February, 1916. By July, 1916 a few German units on the Somme were similarly equipped.

(Above) A German infantryman killed at Beaumont Hamel.

(Below) Crew of a German MG 08 machine-gun. This was the weapon that inflicted such a heavy defeat on the British force, on the morning of 1st July, 1916.

(Above) Two British soldiers operate a Vickers machine-gun near Ovillers. Both men can be seen wearing the primitive anti-gas hoods of the period, July, 1916.

(Below) Getting to grips with cold steel: An artist's impression of the frantic scenes as British infantry rush a German trench on the Somme.

These men can be seen bringing up ammunition under fire in a Somme advance. Resupplying the cumbersome ammunition was a arduous but vital job once the battle was underway.

(Above) After the attack: Depleted ranks assemble for roll-call in the captured trenches on 1ˢᵗ July, 1916. The first day on the Somme saw a staggering 57,470 British casualties including 19,240 men killed.

(Below) A shell hole between Montauban and Carnoy is filled with the bodies of dead German soldiers.

Carrying in the wounded under fire: This man is thought to have brought in twenty of his wounded comrades from No Man's Land.

(Above) Regimental stretcher-bearers bringing wounded in from the battlefield to the collecting posts. This was a difficult but essential task which was aided by a number of unofficial trenches.

(Below) An injured soldier being carried through a trench under shell fire. The wounded man died 30 minutes after reaching the trenches.

(Above) British troops at the entrance to a German dug-out in Danzig Alley, Fricourt, July, 1916.

(Below) Entrance to a German officer's dug-out showing the quality of protection over its doorway and the great depth of these positions.

(Above) During afternoon of the first day of the Battle of the Somme, the Seaforth Highlanders assemble for roll-call near Beaumont Hamel.

(Below) British troops digging in near Mametz Wood, July, 1916.

(Above) *The southern road near Mametz Wood.*

(Below) *These British troops are pictured at Mametz Wood, beginning the arduous and interminable task of digging fresh trenches.*

Service Corps park, with its lines of roughly made stables. At one part of the journey a 15-inch gun let fly just over the road. We had endured quite enough noise for that day, and I was glad that it did not occur again. From a rather tortuous course through bye-lanes we turned into the main Arras to Doullens road - that long, straight, typical French highway with its avenue of poplars. Shortly afterwards the ambulance drew up outside the Casualty Clearing Station.

The Casualty Clearing Station was situated in the grounds of a château. I believe that the château itself was used as a hospital for those cases which were too bad to be moved farther. We were taken into a long cement-floored building, and laid down in a line of stretchers which ran almost from the doorway up to a screen at the end of the room, behind which dressings and operations were taking place.

On my right was the officer of the K——'s, still fairly cheery, though in a certain amount of pain; on my left lay a rifleman hit in the chest, and very grey about the face; I remember that, as I looked at him, I compared the colour of his face with that of the stomach cases I had seen. A stomach case, as far as I can remember, has an ashen pallor about the face; a lung case has a haggard grey look. Next to him a boy of about eighteen was sitting on his stretcher; he was hit in the jaw, the arms, and the hands, but he calmly took out his pipe, placed it in his blood-stained mouth, and started smoking. I was talking to the officer of the K——'s, when he suddenly fell to groaning, and rolled over on to my stretcher. I tried to comfort him, but words were of no avail. A doctor came along, asked a few questions, and examined the wound, just a small hole in the pit of the stomach; but he looked serious enough about it. The stretcher was lifted up and its tortured occupant borne away behind the screen for an operation. That was the last I saw of a very plucky young fellow. I ate some bread and jam, and drank some tea doled out liberally all down the two lines of stretchers, for another line had formed by now.

My turn came at last, and I was carried off to a table behind the screen, where the wound was probed, dressed, and bandaged tightly, and I had a foretaste of the less pleasant side of hospital life. There were two Army nurses at work on a case next to mine - the first English women

I had seen since I returned from leave six months before. My wound having been dressed, I was almost immediately taken out and put into a motor-lorry. There must have been about nine of us, three rows of three, on the floor of that lorry. I did not find it comfortable, though the best had been done under the circumstances to make it so; neither did the others, many of whom were worse wounded than myself, judging by the groans which arose at every jolt.

We turned down a road leading to the station. Groups of peasants were standing in the village street and crying after us: "Ah! les pauvres blessés! les pauvres Anglais blessés!" These were the last words of gratitude and sympathy that the kind peasants could give us. We drew up behind other ears alongside the hospital train, and the engine-driver looked round from polishing his engine and watched us with the wistful gaze of one to whom hospital train work was no longer a novelty. Walking wounded came dribbling up by ones and twos into the station yard, and were directed into sitting compartments.

The sun was in my eyes, and I felt as if my face was being scorched. I asked an R.A.M.C.N.C.O., standing at the end of the wagon, to get me something to shade my eyes. Then occurred what I felt was an extremely thoughtful act on the part of a wounded man. A badly wounded lance-corporal, on the other side of the lorry, took out his handkerchief and stretched it over to me. When I asked him if he was sure that he did not want it, he insisted on my taking it. It was dirty and blood-stained, but saved me much discomfort, and I thanked him profusely. After about ten minutes our stretchers were hauled out of the lorry. I was borne up to the officers' carriage at the far end of the train. It was a splendidly equipped compartment; and when I found myself between the sheets of my berth, with plenty of pillows under me, I felt as if I had definitely got a stage nearer to England. Some one behind me called my name, and, looking round, I saw my old friend M—— W——, whose party I had nearly run into the night before in that never-to-be-forgotten communication trench, Woman Street. He told me that he had been hit in the wrist and leg. Judging by his flushed appearance, he had something of a temperature.

More wounded were brought or helped in - men as well as officers - till the white walls of the carriage were lined with blood-stained, mud-covered khaki figures, lying, sitting, and propped up in various positions.

The Medical Officer in charge of the train came round and asked us what we should like to drink for dinner.

"Would you like whisky-and-soda, or beer, or lemonade?" he questioned me. This sounded pleasant to my ears, but I only asked for a lemonade.

As the train drew out of the station, one caught a last glimpse of warfare - an aeroplane, wheeling round in the evening sky amongst a swarm of tell-tale smoke-puffs, the explosions of "Archie" shells.

PART II

THE GERMAN EXPERIENCE

BY

SIR PHILIP GIBBS

INTRODUCTION

ALTHOUGH THE QUOTATIONS and letters in this instance are not sourced in the text, this is due to the circumstances in which they were written and the fact that they were intended for publication in newspapers of the time. As readers we therefore have to make a choice whether to trust to the integrity of the writer or to take the whole lot with a pinch of salt and write it off as propaganda for the masses. Fortunately the man responsible for these accounts was an eyewitness with impeccable journalistic credentials. Sir Philip Armand Hamilton Gibbs (1st May, 1877–10th March, 1962) was an English journalist and novelist who served as one of the five official British reporters during the First World War. These pieces all originate from November 1916 and were written following the capture of Beaumont-Hamel by the 51st Highland Division, which took place on 13th November 1916. The significance of the events at Beaumont-Hamel on the first day of the Battle of the Somme was perhaps most strongly felt by the Dominion of Newfoundland which was left with a sense of loss that marked an entire generation. Sir Philip Gibbs was present as a witness to those tragic events.

The son of a civil servant, Gibbs was born in London and received a home education and decided at an early age to develop a career as a writer. His debut article was published in 1894 in the Daily Chronicle; five years later he published the first of many books, Founders of the Empire.

Gibbs received a major boost when he was given the post of literary editor at Alfred Harmsworth's burgeoning tabloid newspaper the *Daily Mail*. He subsequently worked on other prominent newspapers including the *Daily Express*.

One of Gibbs' most noteable journalistic coups was to disprove the claims of Frederick Cook, made in September 1909, to have been being the first man who had reached the north pole. Gibbs didn't trust Cook's "romantic" impressions of his journey into the ice. *The Times* credited Gibbs for "bursting the bubble with one cable to the London newspaper he was representing".

His first attempt at semi-fiction was published in 1909 as *The Street of Adventure*, which recounted the story of the official Liberal newspaper Tribune, founded in 1906 and failing spectacularly in 1908. The paper was founded at vast expense by Franklin Thomasson, MP for Leicester 1906 to 1910 and featured one of the most distinguished staffs ever known in journalism, including H. Brailsford, J. L. Hammond and L. Hobhouse. A man of decidedly liberal views Gibbs took an interest in popular movements of the time, including the suffragettes, publishing a book on the movement in 1910.

With tensions growing in Europe in the years immediately preceding 1914, Gibbs repeatedly expressed a belief that war could be avoided between the Entente and Central Powers. In the event war broke out in Europe in August 1914 and Gibbs secured an early journalistic posting to the Western Front.

It was not long however before the War Office in London resolved to 'manage' popular reporting of the war - i.e. via censorship - and Gibbs was denied permission to remain on the Western Front. Stubbornly refusing to return Gibbs was duly arrested and sent home.

Gibbs was not long out of official favour however. Along with four other men he was officially accredited as a wartime correspondent, his work appearing in the *Daily Telegraph* and *Daily Chronicle*. The price he had to pay for his accreditation was to submit to effective censorship: all of his work was to be vetted by C. E. Montague, formerly of the Manchester Guardian. Although unhappy with the arrangement he nonetheless agreed.

Gibbs' wartime output was prodigious. He not only produced a stream of newspaper articles three of which are reproduced in this volume, but also a series of books: *The Soul of the War* (1915), *The Battle of the Somme* (1917), *From Bapaume to Passchendaele* (1918) and *The Realities of War* (1920). In the latter work Gibbs exacted a form of revenge for the frustration he suffered in submitting to wartime censorship; published after the armistice The Realities of War painted a most unflattering portrait of Sir Douglas Haig, British Commander-in-Chief in France and Flanders, and his General Headquarters. Gibbs also published Now It Can Be Told (1920), an account of his personal experiences in war-torn Europe.

Frustration or no, however, Gibbs gratefully accepted a proffered knighthood at the close of the war. His post-war career continued to be as varied as ever. Embarking shortly after the war upon a lecture tour of the U.S. he also secured the first journalistic interview with a Pope.

Working as a freelance journalist - having resigned from the Daily Chronicle over its support for the Lloyd George government's Irish policy (Gibbs was a Roman Catholic) - he published a series of additional books and articles, including a book of autobiography, Adventures in Journalism (1923).

The outbreak of the Second World War in 1939 brought Gibbs a renewed appointment as a wartime correspondent, this time for the Daily Sketch. This proved a brief stint however and he spent part of the war employed by the British Ministry of Information.

In 1946 he published another volume of memoirs The Pageant of the Years; two further volumes followed in 1949 and 1957: Crowded Company and Life's Adventure, respectively.

He died at Godalming on 10th March 1962.

BOB CARRUTHERS

- CHAPTER I -

THE BRITISH OFFENSIVE AND ITS SIGNIFICANCE

THE CAPTURE OF Beaumont-Hamel, on the 13th day of this month, with more than 6,000 prisoners, after a lull in which the progress of our offensive seemed to have been brought to a halt by weather, was undoubtedly the biggest surprise and shock we have yet given to the German High Command on the Western front.

There may be other surprises of the same kind in store for them - I think there will be - but now it is a good time to look back a little and see as closely as possible what our soldiers have achieved, actually, by so much heroism and so much sacrifice.

In this and one or two articles which may follow I propose to give a picture of the great struggle as it was watched and directed by the German staff, and as it was carried out by the German troops. My narrative is not coloured by imagination or bias. It is coloured only by the red vision of great bloodshed, for the story of the Somme battles on the German side is ghastly and frightful.

From January to May of this year the German Command on the Western front was concentrating all its energy and all its available strength in manpower and gun power upon the attack of Verdun. The Crown Prince had staked all his reputation upon this adventure, which he believed would end in the capture of the strongest French fortress and the destruction of the French armies.

He demanded men and more men until every unit that could be spared from other fronts of the line had been thrown into this furnace. Divisions were called in from other theatres of war, and increased the-strength on the Western front to a total of about 130 divisions.

FEAR OF OUR OFFENSIVE

But the months passed, and Verdun still held out above piles of German corpses on its slopes, and in June Germany looked East and saw a great menace. The Russian offensive was becoming violent. German generals on the Russian fronts sent desperate messages for help. "Send us more men" they said and from the Western front four divisions containing 39-battalions were sent to them.

They must have been sent grudgingly, for now another menace threatened the enemy, and it was on the Western side. The British Armies were getting ready to strike. In spite of Verdun, France still had men enough - withdrawn from a part of the line in which they had been relieved by the British - to co-operate in a new attack.

It was our offensive that the German Command feared most, for they had no exact knowledge of our strength or of the quality of our new troops. They knew that our Army had grown prodigiously since the assault on Loos, nearly a year before.

PREPARING FOR THE BLOW

They had heard of the Canadian reinforcements, and the coming of the Australians, and the steady increase of recruiting in England, and month by month they had heard the louder roar of our guns along the line, and had seen their destructive effect spreading and becoming more terrible. They knew of the steady, quiet, concentration of batteries and divisions on the north and south of the Ancre.

The German Command expected a heavy blow, and prepared for it, but as yet had no knowledge of the driving force behind it. What confidence they had of being able to resist the British attack was based upon the wonderful strength of the lines which they had been digging and fortifying since the autumn of the first year of war - "impregnable positions" they had called them - the inexperience of our troops, their own immense quantity of machine-guns, the courage and skill of their gunners, and their profound belief in the superiority of German Generalship.

In order to prevent espionage during the coming struggle, and to conceal the movement of troops and guns, they ordered the civil populations to be removed from villages close behind their positions, drew cordons of military police across the country, picketed crossroads, and established a network of counter espionage to prevent any leakage of information.

To inspire the German troops with a spirit of martial fervour (not easily aroused to fever-pitch after the bloody losses before Verdun) Orders of the Day were issued to the battalions counselling them to hold fast against the hated English, who stood foremost in the way of peace (that was the gist of a manifesto by Prince Rupprecht of Bavaria, which I found in a dugout at Montauban), and promising them a speedy ending to the war.

GREAT STORES OF MUNITIONS

Great stores of material and munitions were concentrated at railheads and dumps ready to be sent up to the firing lines, and the perfection of German organisation may well have seemed flawless - before the attack began.

The British attack began with the great bombardment several days before July 1st and was a revelation, to the German Command and to the soldiers who had to endure it, of the new and enormous power of our artillery. A number of batteries were unmasked for the first time, and the German gunners found that in "heavies" and in expenditure of high explosives they were outclassed.

They were startled, too, by the skill and accuracy of the British gunners whom they had scorned as "amateurs" and by the daring of our airmen who flew over their lines with the utmost audacity "spotting" for the guns, and registering on batteries, communication trenches, cross-roads, railheads, and every vital point of organisation in the German war-machine working opposite the British lines north and south of the Ancre.

Even before the British infantry had left their trenches at dawn on July 1st German officers behind the firing lines saw with anxiety that all the organisation which had worked so smoothly in times of ordinary trench-warfare was now working only in a hazardous way under a deadly storm of shells.

FATE OF STAFF OFFICERS

Food and supplies of all kinds could not be sent up to front line trenches without many casualties, and sometimes could not be sent up at all. Telephone wires were cut, and communications broken between the front and headquarter staffs. Staff officers sent up to report, were killed on the way to the lines. Troops moving forward from reserve areas came under heavy fire and lost many men before arriving in the support trenches.

Prince Rupprecht of Bavaria, sitting aloof from all this in personal safety, must have known before July 1st that his resources in men and material would be strained to the uttermost by the British attack, but he could take a broader view than men closer to the scene of battle, and taking into account the courage of his troops (he had no need to doubt that), the immense strength of their positions, dug and tunnelled beyond the power of high explosives, the number of his machine-guns, the concentration of his artillery and the rawness of the British troops, he could count up the possible cost and believe that in spite of a heavy price to pay there would be no great break in his lines.

At 7.30 A.M. on July 1st the British infantry left their trenches and attacked on the right angle southwards from Gommecourt, Beaumont Hamel, Thièpval, Ovillers, and La Boiselle, and eastwards from Fricourt, below Mametz and Montauban. For a week the German troops - Bavarians and Prussians - had been crouching in their dug-outs, listening to the ceaseless crashing of the British "drum-fire."

In places like Beaumont Hamel the men down in the deep tunnels - some of them large enough to hold a battalion and a half - were safe as long as they stayed there. But to get in or out was death. Trenches disappeared into a sea of shell-craters, and the men holding them - for some men had to stay on duty there - were blown to fragments of flesh.

Many of the shallower dugouts were smashed in by heavy shells, and officers and men lay dead there as I saw them lying on the first days of July, in Fricourt and Mametz and Montauban.

The living men kept their courage, but below ground, under that tumult of bursting shells, wrote pitiful letters to their people at home describing the horror of those hours. "We are quite shut off from the rest of the world," wrote one of them. "Nothing comes to us. No letters. The English keep such a barrage on our approaches it is terrible. To-morrow evening it will be seven days since this bombardment began. We cannot hold out much longer. Everything is shot to pieces."

TORTURES OF THIRST

Thirst was one of their tortures. In many of the tunnelled shelters there was food enough, but the water could not be sent up. The German soldiers were maddened by thirst. When rain fell many of them crept out and drank filthy water mixed with yellow shell sulphur, and then were killed by high explosives. Other men crept out, careless of death but compelled to drink. They crouched over the bodies of the men who lay above, or in, the shell-holes, and lapped up the puddles, and then crawled down again if they were not hit.

When our infantry attacked at Gommecourt and Beaumont Hamel and Thièpval they were received by waves of machine-gun bullets fired by men who, in spite of the ordeal of our seven days' bombardment, came out into the open now, at the moment of attack which they knew through their periscopes was coming. They brought their guns above the shell-craters of their destroyed trenches under our barrage and served them.

They ran forward even into No Man's Land, and planted their machine-guns there and swept down our men as they charged. Over their heads the German gunners flung a frightful barrage ploughing dreadful gaps in the ranks of our splendid men, who would not be checked, whatever their losses might be, until they had reached the enemy's lines.

OUR OVERWHELMING WAVES

On the left, by Gommecourt and Beaumont Hamel, the British attack did not succeed in all its objectives, though the German line was pierced, and if this had been all the line of battle the enemy's Generals at the end of that day might have said, "It is well. We can hold them back."

But southward the "impregnable" lines were smashed by a tide of British soldiers as sand castles are overwhelmed by the waves. Our men swept up to Fricourt, struck straight up to Montauban on the right, captured it, and flung a loop round Mametz village.

For the German Generals, receiving their reports with great difficulty because runners were killed and telephones broken, the question was, "How will these British troops fight in the open after their first assault? How will our men stand between the first line and the second?"

As far as the German troops were concerned there were no signs of cowardice, or "low moral" as we call it more kindly, in those early days of the struggle. They fought with a desperate courage, holding on to positions in rearguard actions when our guns were slashing them, and when our men were getting near to them making us pay a heavy price for every little copse or gully or section of trench, and above all serving their machine-guns at La Boiselle, Ovillers, above Fricourt, round Contalmaison, and at all points of their gradual retreat, with a splendid obstinacy until they were killed or captured. But they could not check our men, or stop their progress.

REVISED OPINIONS

After the first week of battle the German General Staff had learnt the truth about the qualities of those British "New Armies" which had been mocked and caricatured in German comic papers. They learnt that these "amateur soldiers" had the qualities of the finest troops in the world - not only extreme valour but skill and cunning, not only a great power of endurance under the heaviest fire, but a spirit of attack which was terrible in its effect.

They were great bayonet fighters. Once having gained a bit of earth or a ruined village nothing would budge them unless they could be blasted out by gunfire. General Sixt von Arnim put down some candid notes in his report to Prince Rupprecht.

"The English infantry shows great dash in attack, a factor to which immense confidence in its overwhelming artillery greatly contributes… It has shown great tenacity in defence. This was especially noticeable in the case of small parties which when once established with machine guns in the corner of a wood or a group of houses were very difficult to drive out."

The German losses were piling up. The great agony of the German troops under our shellfire was reaching unnatural limits of torture. The early prisoners I saw - Prussians and Bavarians of the 14th Reserve Corps - were nerve-broken, and told frightful stories of the way in which their regiments had been cut to pieces. The German Generals had to fill up the gaps, to put new barriers of men against the waves of British infantry. They flung new troops into the line, called up hurriedly from reserve depots.

STAFF DEMORALISATION

But now, for the first time, their staff work showed signs of disorder and demoralisation. When the Prussian Guards reserves were brought up from Valenciennes to counter-attack at Contalmaison they were sent on to the battlefield without maps or local guides, and walked straight into our barrage. A whole battalion was cut to pieces, and many others suffered frightful things. Some of the prisoners told me that they had lost three-quarters of their number in casualties and our troops advanced over heaps of killed and wounded.

The 122nd Bavarian regiment in Contalmaison was among those, which suffered horribly. Owing to our ceaseless gunfire they could get no food supplies and no water. The dugouts were crowded, so that they had to take turns to get into these shelters, and outside our shells were bursting over every yard of ground.

"Those who went outside," a prisoner told me, "were killed or wounded. Some of them had their heads blown off, and some of them had both their legs torn off, and some of them their arms. But we went on taking turns in the hole, although those who went outside knew that it was their turn to die, most likely. At last most of those who came into the hole were wounded, some of them badly, so that we lay in blood." It is one little picture in a great panorama of bloodshed.

The German Command was not thinking much about the human suffering of its troops. It was thinking, necessarily, of the next defensive line upon which they would have to fall back if the pressure of the British offensive could be maintained - the Longueval-Bazentin-Pozières line. It was getting nervous. Owing to the enormous efforts made in the Verdun offensive the supplies of ammunition were not adequate to the enormous demand.

The German gunners were trying to compete with the British in continuity of bombardments and the shells were running short. Guns were wearing out under this incessant strain, and it was difficult to replace them. General von Gallwitz received reports of "an alarmingly large number of bursts in the bore, particularly in field guns."

General von Arnim complained that "reserve supplies of ammunition were only available in very small quantities." The German telephone system proved "totally inadequate in consequence of the development which the fighting took." The German air service was surprisingly weak, and the British airmen had established a complete mastery.

"The numerical superiority of the enemy's airmen," noted General von Arnim, "and the fact that their machines were better made, became disagreeably apparent to us, particularly in their direction of the enemy's artillery fire and in bomb-dropping."

FEAR OF BRITISH BAYONETS

On July 15, one of the greatest days in the history of the Somme battles, the British troops broke the German second line at Longueval and the Bazentins, and inflicted great losses upon the enemy, who fought with their usual courage until the British bayonets were among them.

A day or two later the fortress of Ovillers fell, and the remnants of the garrison - 150 strong - after a desperate and gallant resistance in ditches and tunnels where they had fought to the last, surrendered with honour.

Then began the long battle of the woods - Devil's Wood, High Wood, Trones Wood - continued through August with most fierce and bloody fighting, which ended in our favour and forced the enemy back, gradually but steadily, in spite of the terrific bombardments which filled those woods with hell-fire, and the constant counter-attacks delivered by the Germans.

" Counter-attack!" came the order from the German Staff - and battalions of men marched out obediently to certain death, sometimes with incredible folly on the part of their commanding officers, who ordered these attacks to be made without the slightest chance of success.

CRY OF AGONY

In all the letters written during those weeks of fighting and captured by us from dead or living men there is one great cry of agony and horror.

"I stood on the brink of the most terrible days of my life," wrote one of them. "They were those of the battle of the Somme. It began with a night attack on August 13-14. The attack lasted till the evening of the

18th, when the English wrote on our bodies in letters of blood: 'It is all over with you.' A handful of half-mad, wretched creatures, worn out in body and mind, were all that was left of a whole battalion. We were that handful."

The losses of many of the German battalions were staggering, and by the middle of August the moral of the troops was severely shaken. So far as I can ascertain, the 117th Division by Pozières suffered very heavily. The 11th Reserve and 157th Regiments each lost nearly three-quarters of their effectives. The IX Reserve Corps had also lost heavily. The 9th Reserve Jaeger Battalion also lost about three-quarters, the 84th Reserve and 86th Reserve over half. On August 10 the 16th Division had six battalions in reserve.

By August 19, owing to the large number of casualties, the greater part of those reserves had been absorbed into the front and support trenches, leaving as available reserves two exhausted battalions.

The weakness of the division and the absolute necessity of reinforcing it led to the 15th Reserve Infantry Regiment (2nd Guards Division) being brought up to strengthen the right flank in the Leipzig salient. This regiment had suffered casualties to the extent of over 50 per cent, west of Pozières during the middle of July, and showed no eagerness to return to the fight. These are but a few examples of what was happening along the whole of the German front on the Somme.

EXHAUSTED DIVISIONS

It became apparent by the end of August that the enemy was having considerable difficulty in finding fresh troops to relieve his exhausted divisions, and that the wastage was faster than the arrival of fresh troops. It was also noticeable that he left divisions in the line until incapable of further effort rather than relieving them earlier so that after resting they might again be brought on to the battlefield. The only conclusion to be drawn from this was that the enemy had not sufficient formations available to make the necessary reliefs.

In July three of these exhausted divisions were sent to the East, their place being taken by two new divisions, and in August three more exhausted divisions were sent to Russia, eight new divisions coming to the Somme front. The British and French offensive was drawing in all the German reserves and draining them of their life's blood.

"We entrained at Savigny," wrote a man of one of these regiments, "and at once knew our destination. It was our old Blood-bath - the Somme."

In many letters this phrase was used. The Somme was called the "Bath of Blood" by the German troops who waded across its shell-craters, and in the ditches which were heaped with their dead. But what I have described is only the beginning of the battle, and the bath was to be filled deeper in the months that followed.

(Above) The Battle of Morval: Supporting troops following the first line of attack, 25th September, 1916.

(Below) A British wiring party off to consolidate newly-won terrain on the Somme front.

(Above) The shallow dug outs of a front line trench are occupied by the men of the Border Regiment, at rest near Thièpval Wood.

(Below) A Lewis gun captured by the Germans is transported away in triumph, July, 1916.

(Above) Sunday on the Somme front: An impromptu service while the nearby guns continue to fire.

(Below) The scene at a British dressing station near 'White City' during the battle.

(Above) R.A.M.C. men conveying wounded from the collecting posts to the advanced dressing station.

(Below) The Battle of Bazentin Ridge: Refreshment caravans were pressed into use for the walking wounded, 14th July, 1916. The left hand one carries the sign of the 9th (Scottish) Division.

(Above) Near Ginchy, British wounded troops are attended to, despite the enemy shells exploding in the background, 14th September, 1916.

(Below) Wounded German soldiers are handed water, 30th July, 1916.

(Above) At a dressing station situated near the front, wounded British soldiers are treated and given immediate first aid and water.

(Below) The first batch of German prisoners is escorted into captivity on 1ˢᵗ July, 1916.

(Above) German prisoners proceeding to internment via a supporting trench.

(Below) Captured German soldiers who were lightly wounded in the fighting, are pictured through barbed wire at near Morlancourt.

(Above) The spoils of war outside a captured German machine-gun post near Mametz, August, 1916.

(Below) Mr. J. Irvine, 'Morning Post' and Mr. Philip Gibbs, 'Daily Chronicle' (right), watching an aerial combat from a trench, 20th September, 1916.

(Above) The destruction caused in Deliville Wood is shown here as ammunition limbers of the 35th Field Battery, the Royal Field Artillery pass through.

(Below) A young German soldier engaged in the Battle of the Somme. Only a few units had received the Stahlhelm by the beginning of the battle - most still wore the leather Pickelhaube.

(Above) Returning from the front are a wounded Grenadier Guardsman and a diminutive German prisoner. Taken near Ginchy, 25th September, 1916.

(Below) Then and Now: A soldier of the Border Regiment is imposed on to an image of the trenches as they are today. These works were uncovered by the La Boisselle study group.

(Above) The view from the German front line trenches at La Boisselle looking towards Albert. The spire on the right of the photograph was capped by the famous hanging statue of the Virgin Mary.

(Below) The view over 'Mash Valley' gives a clear indication of the open nature of the terrain.

(Above) The outlook today of the terrain over which the men of the Royal Newfoundland Regiment attacked on the morning of the 1ˢᵗ July, 1916.

(Below) A short service of remembrance is held annually at the Lochnagar mine crater at 7.20 A.M. on 1ˢᵗ July. The huge scale of the explosion can still be clearly seen by the tiny figures against the skyline.

(Above) The British cemetery near Ovillers is one of dozens which mark the landscape of the Somme region. The scale of the sacrifice is clearly conveyed by the size of this site.

(Below) The German cemetery at Fricourt is the last resting place of some 12,000 German soldiers.

(Above) *This photograph shows the small, secluded cemetery which holds the bodies of the men of the Dorset Regiment who fell on 1ˢᵗ July, 1916.*

(Below) *The headstones mark the last resting place of the men of the Gordon regiment. It is the corpses of these men which can be seen in the famous documentary film of the battle.*

(Above) The Sunken Lane in No Man's Land near Beaumont Hamel which was occupied by the men of the 1st Battalion of the Lancashire Fusiliers on 1st July, 1916.

(Below) The trenches are uncovered once more by the La Boiselle study group.

(Above) The heroic deeds of the 36ᵗʰ 'Ulster' Division are commemorated today by this gracious monument. Every year on 1ˢᵗ July a service of commemoration is held on this spot.

(Below) The memorial to the lost at Thièpval is testament to the thousands of men who left no remains.

- CHAPTER II -

"THE BATH OF BLOOD"

BEFORE THE ENDING of the first phase of the Battles of the Somme - the second phase begins, I imagine, with our great advance on September 15 from the Pozières-Longueval-Guillemont line - the German troops had invented a terrible name to describe this great ordeal; it was "The Blood Bath of the Somme."

The name and the news could not be hidden from the people of Germany, who had already been chilled with horror by the losses at Verdun, nor from the soldiers of reserve regiments quartered in French and Belgian towns like Valenciennes, St. Quentin, Cambrai, Lille, Bruges, and as far back as Brussels, waiting to go to the front, nor from the civil population of those towns held for two years by their enemy - these blonde young men who lived in their houses, marched down their streets, and made love to their women.

The news was brought down from the Somme front by Red Cross trains, arriving in endless succession, and packed with maimed and mangled men. German military policemen formed cordons round the railway stations, pushed back civilians who came to stare with somber eyes at these blanketed bundles of living flesh, but when the ambulances rumbled through the streets towards the hospitals - long processions of them, with the soles of men's boots turned up over the stretchers on which they lay quiet and stiff - the tale was told though no word was spoken.

BAD NEWS BADLY TAKEN

The tale of defeat, of great losses, of grave and increasing anxiety, was told clearly enough - as I have read in captured letters - by the faces of German officers who went about in these towns behind the lines with gloomy looks, and whose tempers, never of the sweetest, became irritable and unbearable so that the soldiers hated them for all this cursing and bullying. A certain battalion commander has a nervous breakdown because he has to meet his colonel in the morning.

"He is dying with fear and anxiety," writes one of his comrades. Other men, not battalion commanders, are even more afraid of their superior officers, upon whom this bad news from the Somme has an evil effect.

The bad news was spread by divisions taken out of the line and sent back to rest. The men reported that their battalions had been cut to pieces. Some of their regiments had lost three-quarters of their strength. They described the frightful effect of the British artillery - the smashed trenches, the shell-craters, the great horror.

It is not good for the moral of men who are just going up there to take their turn.

The man who was afraid of his colonel "sits all day long writing home with the picture of his wife and children before his eyes." He is afraid of other things.

BAVARIANS BEAR THE BRUNT

Bavarian soldiers quarrelled with Prussians, accused them (unjustly) of shirking the Somme battlefields and leaving the Bavarians to go to the blood-bath.

"All the Bavarian troops are being sent to the Somme (this much is certain, you can see no Prussians there), and this in spite of the losses the 5th Bavarian Corps suffered recently at Verdun! And how we did suffer!… It appears that we are in for another turn, at least the 5th Bavarian Division. Everybody has been talking about it for a long time. To the devil with it! Every Bavarian regiment is being sent into it, and it's a swindle."

It was in no cheerful mood that men went away to the Somme battlefields. Those battalions of grey-clad men entrained without any of the old enthusiasm with which they had gone to earlier battles. Their gloom was noticed by the officers.

"Sing, you sheep's heads, sing!" they shouted.

They were compelled to sing, by order.

"In the afternoon," wrote a man of the 18th Reserve Division, "we had to go out again: we were to learn to sing. The greater part did not join in, and the song went feebly. Then we had to march round in a circle and sing, and that went no better.

"After that we had an hour off, and on the way back to billets we were to sing 'Deutschland uber Alles,' but this broke down completely. One never hears songs of the Fatherland any more."

They were silent, grave-eyed men who marched through the streets of French and Belgian towns to be entrained for the Somme front, for they had forebodings of the fate before them. Yet none of their forebodings were equal in intensity of fear to the frightful reality into which they were flung.

The journey to the Somme front on the German side was a way of terror, ugliness, and death. Not all the imagination of morbid minds searching obscenely for foulness and blood in the great deep pits of human agony could surpass these scenes along the way to the German lines round Courcelette, and Flers, Gueudecourt, Morval and Lesboeufs.

Many times, long before a German battalion had arrived near the trenches, it was but a collection of nerve-broken men bemoaning losses already suffered far behind the lines and filled with hideous apprehension. For British long-range guns were hurling high explosives into distant villages, barraging cross-roads, reaching out to railheads and ammunition dumps, while British airmen were on bombing flights over railway stations and rest-billets and high roads down which the German troops came marching at Cambrai, Bapaume, in the valley between Irles and Warlencourt, at Ligny-Thilloy, Busigny, and many other places on the lines of route.

BOMBED BY OUR AIRMEN

German soldiers arriving at Cambrai by train found themselves under the fire of a single aeroplane, which flew very low and dropped bombs. They exploded with heavy crashes, and one bomb hit the first carriage behind the engine, killing and wounding several men.

A second bomb hit the station buildings, and there was a great clatter of broken glass, the rending of wood and the fall of bricks. All lights went out, and the German soldiers groped about in the darkness amidst the splinters of glass and the fallen bricks, searching for the wounded by the sound of their groans.

It was but one scene along the way to that bloodbath through which they had to wade to the trenches of the Somme.

Flights of British aeroplanes circled over the villages on the way. At Grevilliers, in August, eleven 112-16 bombs fell in the market square so that the centre of the village collapsed in a state of ruin, burying soldiers billeted there. Every day the British airmen paid these visits, meeting the Germans far up the roads on their way to the Somme, and swooping over them like a flying Death.

Even on the march in open country the German soldiers tramping silently along - not singing in spite of orders - were bombed and shot at by these British aviators, who flew down very low, pouring out streams of machine-gun bullets.

The Germans lost their nerve at such times, and scattered into the ditches, falling over each other, struck and cursed by their "unteroffizieren," and leaving their dead and wounded in the roadway.

CHAOS ON THE ROADS

As the roads went nearer to the battlefields they were choked with the traffic of war, with artillery and transport wagons and horse ambulances, and always thousands of grey men marching up to the lines, or back from them, exhausted and broken after many days in the fires of hell up there.

Officers sat on their horses by the roadside directing all the traffic with the usual swearing and cursing, and rode alongside the transport wagons and the troops, urging them forward at a quicker pace, because of stern orders received from headquarters demanding quicker movement. The reserves, it seemed, were desperately wanted up in the lines. The English were attacking again.

God alone knew what was happening. Regiments had lost their way. Wounded were pouring back. Officers had gone mad… Into the midst of all this turmoil shells fell - shells from long-range guns. Transport wagons were blown to bits. The bodies and fragments of artillery horses lay all over the roads. Men lay dead or bleeding under the debris of gun-wheels and broken bricks.

Above all the noise of this confusion and death in the night the hard, stern voices of German officers rang out, and German discipline prevailed and men marched on to greater perils.

IN THE SHELL ZONE

They were in the shell zone now, and sometimes a regiment on the march was tracked all along the way by British gunfire directed from aeroplanes and captive balloons. It was the fate of a captured officer I met who had detrained at Bapaume for the trenches at Contalmaison. At Bapaume his battalion was hit by fragments of 12-inch shells.

Nearer to the line they came under the fire of 8-inch and 6-inch shells. Four-point-sevens found them somewhere by Bazentin. At Contalmaison they marched into a barrage, and here the officer was taken prisoner. Of his battalion there were few men left.

It was so with the 3rd Jaeger Battalion, ordered up hurriedly to make a counter-attack near Flers. They suffered so heavily on the way to the trenches that no attack could be made. The stretcher-bearers had all the work to do.

The way up to the trenches became more tragic as every kilometer was passed, until the stench of corruption was wafted on the wind, so that men were sickened and tried not to breathe, and marched hurriedly to get on the lee side of its foulness. They walked now through places, which had once been villages, but were sinister ruins where death lay in wait for German soldiers.

"It seems queer to me," wrote one of them, "that whole villages close to the front look as flattened as a child's toy run over by a steam roller. Not one stone remains on another. The streets are one line of shell-holes. Add to that the thunder of the guns, and you will see with what feelings we come into the line - into trenches where for months shells of all calibre have rained... Flers is a scrap-heap."

Again and again men lost their way up to the lines. The reliefs could only be made at night, lest they should be discovered by British airmen and British gunners, and even if these German soldiers had trench-maps the guidance was but little good when many trenches had been smashed in, and only shell-craters could be found.

"In the front line of Flers," wrote one of these Germans, "the men were only occupying shell-holes. Behind there was the intense smell of putrefaction, which filled the trench - almost unbearably. The corpses lie either quite insufficiently covered with earth on the edge of the trench or quite close under the bottom of the trench, so that the earth lets the stench through. In some places bodies lie quite uncovered in a trench recess, and no one seems to trouble about them. One sees horrible pictures - here an arm, here a foot, here a head, sticking out of the earth. And these are all German soldiers - heroes!

"IMPOSSIBLE TO HOLD OUT"

"Not far from us at the entrance to a dug-out nine men were buried, of whom three were dead. All along the trench men kept on getting buried. What had been a perfect trench a few hours before was in parts completely blown in... The men are getting weaker. It is impossible to hold out any longer. Losses can no longer be reckoned accurately. Without a doubt many of our people are killed."

That is only one out of thousands of such gruesome pictures, true as the death they described, which have gone home to German homes during the Battles of the Somme. These German soldiers are grand letter writers, and men sitting in wet ditches, in "fox-holes," as they call their dug-outs, "up to my waist in mud," as one of them described, scribbled pitiful things which they hoped might reach their people at home, as a voice from the dead. For they had had little hope of escape from the "blood-bath."

"When you get this I shall be a corpse," wrote one of them, and one finds the same foreboding in many of these documents.

WRITTEN BY ONE NOW DEAD

Even the lucky ones who could get some cover from the incessant bombardment by English guns began to lose their nerves after a day or two. They were always in fear of British infantry, sweeping upon them suddenly behind the "Trommel-feuer," rushing their dugouts with bombs and bayonets. Sentries became "jumpy" and signalled attacks when there were no attacks. The gas-alarm was sounded constantly by the clang of a bell in the trench, and men put on their heavy gas masks and sat in them until they were nearly stifled.

Here is a little picture of life in a German dugout near the British lines, written by a man now dead.

"The telephone bell rings. 'Are you there? Yes, here's Nau's battalion.' 'Good. That is all.' Then that ceases, and now the wire is in again, perhaps for the 25th or 30th time. Thus the night is interrupted, and now they come, alarm messages, one after the other, each more terrifying than the other, of enormous losses through the bombs and shells of the enemy, of huge masses of troops advancing upon us, of all possible possibilities, such as a man broken down and tortured by the terrors of the day can invent. Our nerves quiver. We clench our teeth. None of us can forget the horrors of the night."

Heavy rain fell, and the dugouts became wet and filthy.

"Our sleeping-places were full of water. We had to try and bail out the trenches with cooking dishes. I lay down in the water with G… We were to have worked on dugouts, but not a soul could do any more. Only a few sections got coffee. Mine got nothing at all. I was frozen in every limb, poured the water out of my boots, and lay down again."

GENERAL STAFF ALARMED

The German generals and their staffs could not be quite indifferent to all this welter of human suffering among their troops, in spite of the cold scientific spirit with which they regard the problem of war. The agony of the individual soldier would not trouble them. There is no war without agony. But the psychology of masses of men had to be considered, because it affects the efficiency of the machine.

As I shall show, the German General Staff on the Western front were becoming seriously alarmed by the declining moral of their infantry under the increasing strain of the British attacks, and adopted stern measures to cure it. But they could not hope to cure the heaps of German dead who were lying on the battlefields, nor the maimed men who were being carried back to the dressing stations, nor to bring back the prisoners taken in droves by the French and British troops.

Before the attack on the Flers line, the capture of Thièpval, and the German debacle at Beaumont-Hamel the enemy's command was already filled with a grave anxiety at the enormous losses of its fighting strength, was compelled to adopt new expedients for increasing the number of its divisions. It was forced to withdraw troops badly needed on other fronts, and, as I shall point out, the successive shocks of the British offensive reached as far as Germany itself, so that the whole of its recruiting system had to be revised to fill up the gaps torn out of the German ranks.

- CHAPTER III -

THE BREAKING
OF MORAL

ALL THROUGH JULY and August the enemy's troops fought with great and stubborn courage, defending every bit of broken woodland, every heap of bricks that was once a village, every line of trenches smashed by heavy shell-fire, with obstinacy.

It is, indeed, fair and just to say that throughout these battles of the Somme up to the present day our men have fought against an enemy hard to beat, grim and resolute, and inspired sometimes with the courage of despair, which is hardly less dangerous than the courage of hope.

The Australians who struggled to get the high ground at Pozières did not have an easy task. The enemy made many counter attacks against them. All the ground hereabouts was so smashed that the earth became finely powdered, and it was the arena of bloody fighting at close quarters which did not last a day or two, but many weeks. Mouquet Farm was like the Phoenix, which rose again out of its ashes.

In its tunnelled ways German soldiers hid and came out to fight our men in the rear long after the site of the farm was in our hands. Delville Wood was a living horror, which could not for a long time be cleared of its devilish properties. Our shell fire slashed through its broken trees and our men fought their way over its barricades of fallen logs and dead bodies, but the German soldier crept back with machine-guns, and would not give up this place of dreadful memory. It was not until the beginning of September that it was finally taken.

FIGHTING REARGUARD ACTIONS

But the German troops were fighting what they now knew to be a losing battle. They were fighting rearguard actions, trying to gain time for the hasty digging of ditches behind them, trying to sell their lives at the highest price.

They lived not only under incessant gun-fire, gradually weakening their nerve power, working a physical as well as a moral change in them, but in constant terror of British attacks.

They could never be sure of safety at any hour of the day or night, even in their deepest dugouts. The British varied their times of attack. At dawn, at noon, when the sun was reddening in the west, just before the dusk, in pitch darkness even, the steady, regular bombardment that had never ceased all through the days and nights would concentrate into the great tumult of sudden drum fire, and presently waves of men - English or Scottish or Irish, Australians or Canadians - would be sweeping on to them and over them, rummaging down into the dugouts with bombs and bayonets, gathering up prisoners, quick to kill if men were not quick in surrender.

In this way Thièpval was encircled so that the garrison there - the I Both Regiment, who had held it for two years - knew that they were doomed. In this way Guillemont and Ginchy fell, so that in the first place not a man out of 2,000 men escaped to tell the tale of horror in German lines, and in the second place there was no long fight against the Irish, who stormed it in a wild, fierce rush, which even machine-guns could not check.

SHORTAGE OF MUNITIONS

The German General Staff was getting flurried, grabbing at battalions from short parts of the line, disorganising its divisions under the urgent need of flinging in men to stop this rot in the lines, ordering counter-attacks which were without any chance of success, so that thin waves of men came out into the open, as I have seen them myself, to be swept down by scythes of bullets which cut them clean to the earth. Before September 15 they hoped that the British offensive was wearing itself out. It seemed to them at least doubtful that after the struggle of two and a half months the British troops could still have spirit and strength enough to fling themselves against new lines.

Their own reserves of strength were failing to keep pace with the tremendous strain upon the whole machinery of their organisation.

Many of their guns had worn out, and could not be replaced quickly enough.

Many batteries had been knocked out in their emplacements along the line of Bazentin and Longueval before the artillery was drawn back to Grandcourt and a new line of safety.

Battalion commanders clamoured for greater supplies of hand grenades, entrenching tools, trench-mortars, signal rockets, and all kinds of fighting material enormously in excess of all previous requirements.

The difficulties of dealing with the wounded, who littered the battlefields and choked the roads with the traffic of ambulances became increasingly severe owing to the dearth of horses for transport and the longer range of British guns which had been brought far forward.

The German General Staff studied its next lines of defence away through Courcelette, Martinpuich, Lesboeufs, Morval, and Combles, and they did not look too good, but, with luck and the courage of German soldiers, and the exhaustion - surely those fellows were exhausted! - of British troops good enough.

TIDAL WAVE AND "TANKS"

On September 15 the German command had another great shock. The whole line of the British troops on the Somme front south of the Ancre rose out of their trenches and swept over the German defences in a great tide.

The defences broke hopelessly, and the waves dashed through. Here and there, as on the German left at Morval and Lesboeufs, the bulwarks stood for a time, but the British pressed against them and round them. On the German right, below the little river of the Ancre, Courcelette fell, and Martinpuich, and High Wood, which the Germans desired to hold at all costs, and had held against incessant attacks by great concentration of artillery, was captured and left behind by the London men. A new engine of war had come as a demoralising influence among German troops, spreading terror among them.

It was the first day out of those fantastic monsters the Tanks, strange and horrible in their surprise, very deadly in their action against machine-gun emplacements, not stopped by trenches or barbed-wire, or tree stumps, or refuse heaps of fallen houses. For the first time the Germans were outwitted in inventions of destruction, they who had been foremost in all engines of death.

It was the moment of real panic in the German lines - a panic reaching back from the troops to the High Command.

BLACK DAYS FOR THE ENEMY

Ten days later, on September 25, when the British made a new advance - all this time the French were pressing forward too but that is no part of my story - Combles was evacuated without a fight and with a litter of dead in its streets; Gueudecourt, Lesboeufs, and Morval were lost by the Germans; and a day later Thièpval, the greatest fortress position next to Beaumont Hamel, fell, with all its garrison taken prisoners.

They were black days in the German Headquarters, where Staff officers heard the news over their telephones, and sent stern orders to artillery commanders and divisional Generals, and, after dictating new instructions that certain trench systems must be held at whatever price, heard that already they were lost.

It was at this time that the moral of the German troops on the

Somme front showed most signs of breaking. In spite of all their courage the ordeal had been too hideous for them, and in spite of all their discipline, the iron discipline of the German soldier, they were on the edge of revolt. The intimate and undoubted facts of this break in the moral of the enemy's troops during this period reveal a pitiful picture of human agony.

"MERE MURDER"

"We are now fighting on the Somme with the English," wrote a man of the 17th Bavarian Regiment. "You can no longer call it war. It is mere murder. We are at the focal point of the present battle in Foureaux Wood (near Guillemont). All my previous experience in this war - the slaughter at Ypres and the battle in the gravel-pit at Hulluch - are the purest child's play compared with this massacre, and that is much too mild a description. I hardly think they will bring us into the fight again, for we are in a very bad way."

"From September 12 to 27 we were on the Somme," wrote a man of the 10th Bavarians, "and my regiment had 1,500 casualties."

A detailed picture of the German losses under our bombardment is given in the diary of an officer captured in a trench near Flers, and dated September 22.

"The four days ending September 4 spent in the trenches were characterised by a continual enemy bombardment that did not abate for a single instant.

"The enemy had registered on our trenches with light, as well as medium and heavy batteries, notwithstanding that he had no direct observation from his trenches, which lie on the other side of the summit. His registering was done by his excellent air-service, which renders perfect reports of everything observed.

"During the first day, for instance, whenever the slightest movement was visible in our trenches during the presence, as is usually the case, of enemy aircraft flying as low as 300-400 yards, a heavy bombardment of the particular section took place. The very heavy losses during the first day brought about the resolution to evacuate the trenches during the daytime. Only a small garrison was left, the remainder withdrawing to a part of the line on the left of the Martinpuich-Pozières road.

ENGLISH AIRMEN'S SUPERIORITY

"The signal for a bombardment by heavies was given by the English aeroplanes. On the first day we tried to fire by platoons on the aeroplanes, but a second aeroplane retaliated by dropping bombs and firing his machine-gun at our troops. Our own airmen appeared only once for a short time behind our lines.

"While enemy aeroplanes are observing from early morning till late at night our own hardly ever venture near. The opinion is that our trenches cannot protect troops during a barrage of the shortest duration owing to lack of dugouts.

"The enemy understands how to prevent with his terrible barrage the bringing up of building material and even how to hinder the work itself. The consequence is that our trenches are always ready for an assault on his part. Our artillery, which does occasionally put a heavy barrage on the enemy trenches at a great expense of ammunition, cannot cause similar destruction to him. He can bring his building material up, can repair his trenches as well as build new ones, can bring up rations and ammunition, and remove the wounded.

"The continual barrage on our lines of communication makes it very difficult for us to ration and relieve our troops, to supply water, ammunition and building material, to evacuate wounded, and causes heavy losses. This and the lack of protection from artillery fire and the weather, the lack of hot meals, the continual necessity of lying still in the same place, the danger of being buried, the long time the wounded have to remain in the trenches, and chiefly the terrible effect of the machine and heavy artillery fire, controlled by an excellent air service, has a most demoralising effect on the troops.

"Only with the greatest difficulty could the men be persuaded to stay in the trenches under those conditions."

MORAL ROT THREATENED

There were some who could not be persuaded to stay, if they could see any chance of deserting or malingering. For the first time on our front the German officers could not trust the courage of their men, nor their loyalty, nor their sense of discipline. All this horror of men blown to bits over living men, of trenches heaped with dead and dying, was stronger than courage, stronger than loyalty, stronger than discipline. A moral rot was threatening to bring the German troops on the Somme front to disaster.

Large numbers of men reported sick, and tried by every kind of trick to be sent back to base hospitals.

In the 4th Bavarian Division desertions were frequent, and several times whole bodies of men refused to go forward into the front line. The moral of men in the 393rd Regiment taken at Courcelette seemed to be very weak. One of the prisoners declared that they gave themselves up without firing a shot because they could trust the English not to kill them.

The platoon commander had gone away, and the prisoner was ordered to alarm the platoon in case of attack, but did not do so on purpose. They did not shoot with rifles or machine-guns, and did not throw bombs.

OFFICERS WHO SHIRKED

Many of the German officers were as demoralised, as the men, shirking their posts in the trenches, shamming sickness, and even leading the way to surrender. Prisoners of the 361st Regiment, which lost 1,300 men in 15 days, told of officers who had refused to take their men up to the front line, and of whole companies who had declined to move when ordered to do so. An officer of the 74ᵗʰ Landwehr Regiment is said by prisoners to have told his men during our preliminary bombardment to surrender as soon as we attacked.

A German regimental Order says: "I must state with the greatest regret that the regiment during this change of position had to take notice of the sad fact that men of four of the companies, inspired by shameful cowardice, left their companies on their own initiative and did not move into line."

Another Order contains the same fact and a warning of what punishment may be meted out:-

"Proofs are multiplying of men leaving the position without permission and hiding at the rear. It is our duty - each at his post - to deal with this fact with energy and success."

Many Bavarians complained that their officers did not accompany them into the trenches, but went down to the hospitals with imaginary diseases. In any case, there was a great deal of real sickness, mental and physical. The ranks were depleted by men suffering from fever, pleurisy, jaundice, and stomach complaints of all kinds, twisted up with rheumatism after lying in water-logged holes, lamed for life by bad cases of trench-foot, and nerve-broken so that they could do nothing but weep.

The nervous cases were the worst, and in greatest number. Many men went raving mad. The shell-shock victims clawed at their mouths unceasingly, or lay motionless like corpses with staring eyes, or trembled in every limb, moaning miserably and afflicted with a great terror.

To the Germans the Somme battlefields were not only shambles but a territory, which the devil claimed as his own for the torture of men's brains and souls before they died in the furnace fires. A spirit of revolt against all this crept into the minds of men who retained their sanity - a revolt against the people who had ordained this vast outrage against God and humanity.

Into their letters there crept bitter, burning words against "the millionaires - who grow rich out of the war," against the high people who live in comfort behind the lines. Letters from home inflamed these thoughts.

It was not good reading for men under shell fire.

"It seems that you soldiers fight so that official stay-at-homes can treat us as female criminals. Tell me, dear husband, are you a criminal when you fight in the trenches, or why do people treat women and children here as such?...

"For the poor here it is terrible, and yet the rich, the gilded ones, the bloated aristocrats, gobble up everything in front of our very eyes... All soldiers - friend and foe - ought to throw down their weapons and go on strike, so that this war which enslaves the people more may cease."

Thousands of letters, all in this strain, were reaching the German soldiers on the Somme, and they did not strengthen the moral of men already victims of terror and despair.

PHYSIC FOR FAINT-HEARTED

Behind the lines deserters were shot in batches. To those in front came Orders of the Day, warning them, exhorting them, commanding them to hold fast.

"To the hesitating and faint-hearted in the regiment," says one of these Orders, "I would say the following:-

"What the Englishman can do the German can do also. Or if, on the other hand, the Englishman really is a better and superior being, he would be quite justified in his aim as regards this war, viz., the extermination of the German. There is a further point to be noted: this is the first time we have been in the line on the Somme, and, what is more, we are there at a time when things are more calm. The English regiments opposing us have been in the firing-line for the second, and, in some cases even the third, time. Heads up, and play the man!"

It was easy to write such documents. It was more difficult to bring up reserves of men and ammunition. The German command was hard pressed by the end of September.

From July 1 to September 8, it has been reckoned, from what I believe was trustworthy information, that fifty-three German divisions in all were engaged against the Allies on the Somme battlefront. Out of these, fourteen were still in the line on September 8.

Twenty-eight had been withdrawn, broken and exhausted, to quieter areas. Eleven more had been withdrawn to rest billets. Under the Allies' artillery fire and infantry attacks the average life of a German division, as a unit fit for service on the Somme was nineteen days. More than two new German divisions had to be brought into the front line every week since the end of June to replace those smashed in the process of resisting the Allied attack. It is now reckoned by competent observers in the field that well over 120 German divisions have been passed through the ordeal of the Somme - this Bath of Blood, as they call it; this number including those which have appeared there more than once.